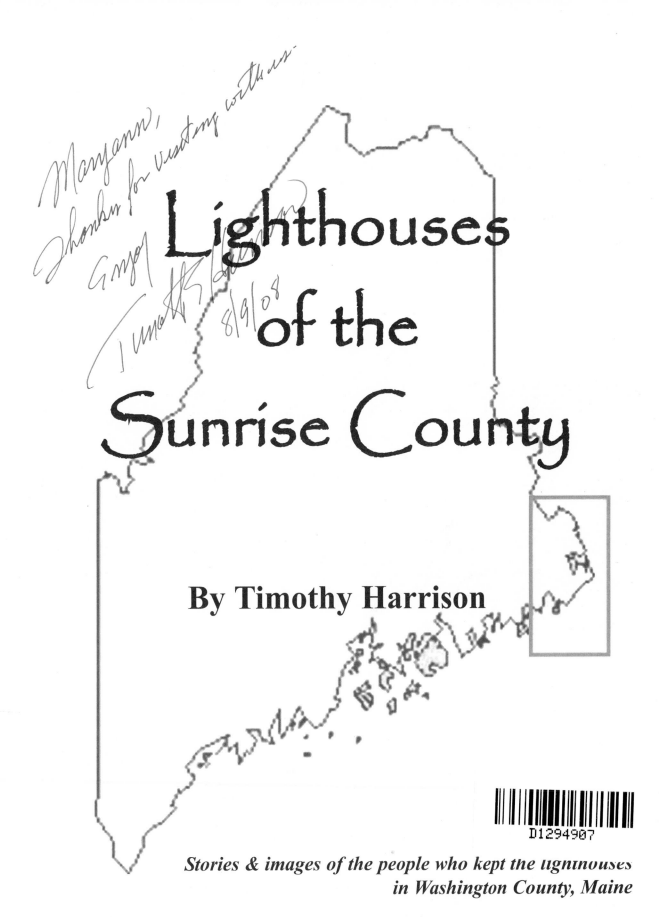

Lighthouses
of the
Sunrise County

By Timothy Harrison

Maryann,
Thanks for visiting with us.
Enjoy
Timothy Harrison
8/9/08

D1294907

Stories & images of the people who kept the lighthouses
in Washington County, Maine

Published and copyrighted by
FogHorn Publishing, Inc.
P.O. Box 250, East Machias, Maine 04630
207-259-2121
www.FogHornPublishing.com

Designed by Kathleen Finnegan.
Covers designed by Grace Gimena.

Printed in the United States of America
First Printing 2008

ISBN-13: 978-0-9778293-2-3
ISBN-10: 0-9778293-2-4

Paul Bradley

Dedication

Lighthouses of the Sunrise County is dedicated in honor of the lighthouse keepers and their family members who served so selflessly and faithfully at the lighthouses in Maine's Washington County. May the legacy they gave us, shine on forever.

Table of Contents

Preface

In the late 1980s, while visiting and photographing lighthouses, Kathleen Finnegan and I realized that, especially at the lesser-known lighthouses, there was an unfilled thirst to learn about the history of lighthouses. We would often wonder, what was life like at the lighthouse? Who lived here? What did the children do? What was the family life like? What hardships did the lighthouse families face? Were there any amazing rescues that took place? What did the people who lived here look like? How did they dress? Were there any recorded memories of life at the lighthouse? While visiting the lighthouses, we would meet many other people that had the same questions that were always left unanswered.

So, in May of 1992, on a whim and a shoestring budget, we launched the first issue of *Lighthouse Digest*, a magazine devoted to lighthouses. Our goal was multifaceted: to locate and tell the stories of lighthouse people so that these memories could be passed down to more than just the descendants, which in many cases, there were none; and to draw public attention to the plight that many of our lighthouses were facing from neglect and abandonment; while also telling the modern stories of what was happening at lighthouses today, so that today's modern history would also be saved for tomorrow's generations. The most challenging part of this search was, and still is, locating the photographs of the lighthouse keepers and their families.

Since the first issue of *Lighthouse Digest* in May of 1992, with only 34 subscribers, the magazine has continued to grow and now has a worldwide audience. We soon realized that we could not publish every photograph we located, while keeping the scope of the magazine appealing to a wide range of public interest.

The only way that a large amount of historical photographs and memories of a given region can be saved, is through a book, such as this, followed by varied selections of more in-depth stories that were located, that could then be later published in the pages of *Lighthouse Digest*.

So, we'd like to think of this book, loaded with never before published images, as an extension of *Lighthouse Digest*.

It would be impossible to print the names of every person who has shared photographs, stories and memories with me over the years to make this book possible. However, I can assure you, that I am thankful to each and everyone one of you who have helped in so many ways. It is because of you, that this vital part of America's lighthouse and maritime history is now saved through the pages of this book, so that future generations can enjoy and learn from what is recorded here, in the pages of *Lighthouses of the Sunrise County*.

Introduction

Lighthouses were built for one purpose only—to save lives. The early citizens of the newly established United States realized the importance of lighthouses and developed the best system of aids to navigation in the world. Lighthouses provided safe transport of our citzens and commerce, which led to the rapid growth and development of the United States of America.

I have often said that one can learn more about early American history by studying lighthouses than from any other single source. Lighthouses constitute the largest group of the oldest standing structures in America.

On August 7, 1789, the First Congress of the United States of America federalized all lighthouses that had been built by the colonies. From 1789 to 1939 our nation's lighthouses operated under various government agencies and had several names such as the United States Lighthouse Establishment, (USLHE), The Lighthouse Board, The Bureau of Lighthouses and the United States Lighthouse Service (USLHS.) However, during most of its existence it was referred to as the "Lighthouse Service."

Further proving the importance of lighthouses, early lighthouse keepers were personally appointed by the President of the United States. In fact our nation's first president, George Washington personally appointed the first lighthouse keepers.

As well as the lighthouse keepers that most people are familiar with, the Lighthouse Service had many other employees who served in a wide variety of positions. Soon the Lighthouse Service grew into a large organization that had its own fleet of vessels, including lighthouse tenders and buoy tenders, as well as its own manufacturing plants, supply depots, fleets of trucks, engineers, clerks, draftsmen, masons, carpenters, inspectors, engineers, machinists, and even its own police force. In fact, at one time the Lighthouse Service had more employees, decentralized outside of Washington DC, than any other government agency. By 1924, the United States Lighthouse Service was the largest lighthouse organization in the world.

However, modern inventions and an ever-changing government brought an end to a way of life that many of the old time lighthouse keepers could never have imagined. The first change came with electricity, followed by trains, changes in shipping routes, ocean buoys, and of course things like radar and sonar. The Lighthouse Service was slow to change and early automation came at a slow pace, mainly from public objections to removing keepers. In the 1930s some discontinued light stations were sold at auction to private owners and have remained in private ownership ever since. Rarely were they offered to the community or local nonprofits.

The biggest and most dramatic change came in 1939 when Congress, under President Franklin Roosevelt's reorganization plan, dissolved the United States Lighthouse Service and merged it into the United States Coast Guard. It was the first time in history that a military branch of the government took over a civilian agency of the government.

The Coast Guard brought a different attitude to the lighthouses and eventually family lighthouse stations were phased out, as were many lighthouses that were no longer needed. When the Coast Guard took over the Lighthouse Service the lighthouse keepers were given a choice of remaining on as civilian keepers or joining the Coast Guard. They split nearly evenly in their decision. However, as civilian keepers retired, they were replaced with Coast Guard personnel. When the Coast Guard took over, orders came from Washington that all items bearing the insignia or emblem of the United States Lighthouse Service were to be destroyed or disposed and were to be replaced by the insignia of the United States Coast Guard. During the transition time and for a number of years thereafter lighthouse keepers were allowed to continue to use the lighthouse insignia on their hats and a few other items.

Eventually all lighthouses were automated and keepers were removed. In many cases discontinued light stations were abandoned and boarded up, others were simply destroyed, some had the keepers' houses destroyed and only the tower was left to display an automated beacon. Some of the more popular lighthouses were used as Coast Guard housing and still are to this day. Some stations were saved early on and became museums and tourist attractions, but this was not the norm. For a variety of reasons, some stations missed the wrecking ball simply by chance.

It wasn't until the late 1980s that many people suddenly realized that we were losing more of our lighthouse history than we were saving and lighthouse preservation groups were formed to try and save some of these structures, but even then, some lighthouses could not be saved.

Of the estimated several thousand lighthouse structures built in the United States approximately only 600 structures still stand today.

The Coast Guard did save some lighthouses, especially those that were in popular areas, and stabilized others, but their limited budget did not allow for historic preservation. Instead, money from its budget was to be used for law enforcement and keeping our nation's waterways safe and clean. Although they still maintain all the aids to navigation, that function, in the case of lighthouses, could be done less expensively through modern aids to navigation and not maintaining historic buildings.

In 1998, the Island Institute in Rockland, Maine, with the cooperation of the United States Coast Guard, developed the Maine Lights Program, which found new preservation owners for many of Maine's Lighthouses. That program led to Congress passing the National Historic Lighthouse Preservation Act of 2000, which essentially allowed lighthouses, as they were being excessed, to be turned over for free to other government agencies or nonprofits. It also allowed for nonprofit preservation groups to compete on equal footing for ownership of a lighthouse. If neither a nonprofit nor other government agency wanted a particular lighthouse, it would then be put up for auction to the highest bidder.

Lighthouses have fascinated people for as nearly as long as the history of them has existed. Many churches use a lighthouse as a symbol to promote the fact that they are a guiding light of God's Word. Lighthouses are often used in the logo of a business as its symbol of strength and security to encourage people to do business with them while implying that they are a solid and safe entity.

Today, more and more people plan their vacations around visiting lighthouses, they fall in love at lighthouses, they meditate at lighthouses, they get married at lighthouses and even have their ashes scattered at lighthouses.

Many lighthouses are now popular tourist attractions, some are bed and breakfasts, and some are private homes. A photo of a lighthouse was put on board the space craft Voyager, which was launched to search out possible alien life in outer space. The idea was to show aliens what a typical lighthouse on earth looked like.

When one thinks of lighthouses, some of the words that often come up are: romance, heroism, bravery, and a different way of life in a simpler and less complicated time. The way of the lighthouse keeper and the families that lived at lighthouses is a way of life than can never again be repeated in history.

Unfortunately, many of the photographs of lighthouse keepers and the families that lived at lighthouses have been destroyed or lost over time, while still others remain to yet be rediscovered. Locating old photographs of lighthouse keepers is a difficult and time-consuming task. Many families of lighthouse keepers are unaware that preservationists and historians are looking for photographs and others may not even know they have them. Even more photographs and documents have been disposed of as people pass through the pages of time and the people in old photographs become unknown and forgotten by their descendants and many have simply and sadly been thrown out with the trash.

This book is not meant to be an in-depth study of lighthouses, how they worked or how they were built, which could fill many volumes. Instead this is a book that has been published to preserve as many photographic images as I could locate of actual people; the lighthouse keepers and their family members and in some cases, today's caretakers of the lighthouses, so that these images, along with a selection of memories and stories, may be preserved in one book for future generations for many years to come. We know there are many other photographs tucked away in attics, family Bibles, libraries and historical societies that we did not find and hopefully this book will lead to the rediscovery of additional photographs that can be used perhaps in a second edition of this book or published in *Lighthouse Digest* magazine.

Never before in the history of lighthouses has such a book ever been published with so many historic images for such a small number of lighthouses. This is the most complete photographic book ever published in history of the lighthouses where the rays of the sun first touch the coast of the United States of America in Washington County, Maine.

Thomas D. Webster was an engineer for the United States Lighthouse Service and was in charge of the crews that worked on most of Maine's lighthouses on various projects such as station improvements, rebuilding, renovations and more. In 1928 he was in charge of the crew that made major renovations to Lubec Channel Lighthouse. He was also in charge of the crew that built the bell tower at Whitlock's Mill Lighthouse. Thomas Webster died in 1948. Unfortunately, the records and documents that he recorded of his work and had been saved from his years in the Lighthouse Service, were thrown out sometime after his death. Photograph courtesy of Thomas Webster II.

This is one of the various types of vessels that the United States Lighthouse Service used. This photograph is of special interest because it is flying the pennant of the United States Lighthouse Service. The U.S. Lighthouse Service pennant was authorized on September 3, 1885. Although the pennant was flown on lighthouse tenders and lightships of the United States Lighthouse Service, it was only allowed to be flown at the one light station in each district that received the highest

marks during the yearly inspections for all lighthouses in a given district. Reportedly, Elson Small, who was a lighthouse keeper at St. Croix and Avery Rock Lighthouse, was awarded the flag more often than any other lighthouse keeper on the Maine coast.

Thomas D. Webster, shown standing to the far left, with a keeper of the Quoddy Head Life Saving Station believed to be Albert H. Myers. The youngster is Webster's son, Earle Webster. The three are in a surfboat used at the Quoddy Head Life Saving Station. Webster's crew did construction work on the life saving station. Photograph courtesy of Thomas Webster II.

Freeman E. Crosby, known as "Hank," is shown here with his mother. He joined the United States Lighthouse Service in 1925 as a Seaman on the Lighthouse Tender *Lotus*. He worked his way up to Quartermaster and served on other lighthouse tenders including the *Azalea*, and like other officers, he was well acquainted with the lighthouse keepers, especially those at Whitlock's Mill, Little River, Avery Rock and Libby Island. He left the United States Lighthouse Service in 1938 to join the Bureau of Marine Inspection. In 1942 the Bureau of Marine Inspection, met a fate similar to the U.S. Lighthouse Service, when it was dissolved and its duties were split between the U.S. Coast Guard and the U.S. Customs Service. Photograph circa 1926, courtesy of Patricia Crocker.

This old, faded image shows Earle Webster on the far left, who followed in his father's footsteps and joined the Lighthouse Service as a machinist and later as a Coast Guard civilian employee. This photograph was taken at Maine's Halfway Rock Lighthouse. When Earle wanted to retire, the Coast Guard wanted him to stay on and offered him the job as the lamplighter of the Dog Island Light in Eastport, Maine, where it is believed he was the last person to care for the light before it was automated.
Photograph courtesy of Thomas Webster II.

The Dog Island Light in Eastport looks much different today, from the wooden pyramid tower that once stood there when it needed to be lighted every night by a lamplighter. The modern skeleton structure there today is solar powered. One of the lamplighters who served the original Dog Island Light was Leonard Clark who died in October 1939. Photograph by Bob Gustafson.

In later years, as technology developed, larger offshore stations, especially those many miles out to sea, were given larger vessels such as the one shown here.

The Lighthouse Tender *Azalea* was one of the various lighthouse vessels that serviced the lighthouses of "Downeast" Maine. It would deliver supplies, fuel, mail and the rotating lighthouse library. Often times it would also bring the lighthouse inspector, a person the keepers and their families always had to be ready for. The officers of the tenders became good friends with the lighthouse keepers and their families.

Ralph Halsey Goddard, (1867-1919), son of Capt. George Halsey Goddard, followed in his father's footsteps and joined the United States Lighthouse Service. He started as a fireman on a lighthouse tender. His story is truly that of a man who worked his was up the ladder. Eventually he was appointed Superintendent of the Lighthouse Service with his office being headquartered in Boston. He held that position until his death.

Harold D. King, shown here with his daughter and wife, at the christening of a Lighthouse Service vessel, was the last Commissioner of the United States Lighthouse Service. A dedicated Lighthouse Service employee, he was appointed to the highest position in 1934, but his tenure was doomed from the day he took office. He fought hard to keep the U.S. Lighthouse Service in existence. In a meeting with President Franklin D. Roosevelt, while trying to save the Lighthouse Service, a heated argument ensued that infuriated the President so much, he shook his fist at King while telling him to accept the inevitable. The Reorganization Act of 1939 dissolved the Lighthouse Service and merged it into the Coast Guard.

1789 Lighthouse Service 1939

This insignia was designed to celebrate the 150th anniversary of the United States Lighthouse Service. Unfortunately, in July of that year the Lighthouse Service was dissolved and merged into the United States Coast Guard, thus ending this historic branch of the government of the United States.

Children of lighthouse keepers, who were stationed at lighthouses where more than one family lived, often became life long friends sharing the same interests. In this case Catherine Freeman (not shown) daughter of James Freeman, who was stationed at Petit Manan and Isles of Shoals lighthouses, and Dorothy Pettegrow, (seated), daughter of Edwin A. Pettegrow, who also served as a keeper at Petit Manan and Isles of Shoals Lighthouses, married the Thaxter brothers, Ronald (standing far left) and Philip, (seated far left.) Also shown here, standing in the middle, is Farrell Pettegrow, son of lighthouse keeper Edwin A. Pettegrow. The other four in the photograph are believed to be members of the Morris family.

Lighthouses
of the
Sunrise County
Washington County • Maine

Avery Rock Lighthouse

Machias Bay — Machias, Maine

Unfortunately, the lighthouse that once stood on desolate Avery Rock, three miles out in Machias Bay, is one of Maine's forgotten and lost lighthouses.

Built in 1875 on a small barren quarter acre rock island, the tower protruded from the center of a square keeper's house that contained six large rooms.

Although there were a few short mentions about Avery Rock written over the years in books or magazines, it was the book, *The Lighthouse Keeper's Wife*, written by Connie Small that provided the most detail about life on the rock. During the fours years she was stationed on the island with her husband, Elson, there was no phone or electricity. Water for drinking, cooking, and washing was collected from the rain in a cistern.

As shipping in the area declined, it was deemed that a manned lighthouse station at Avery Rock was no longer necessary and lighthouse keepers were removed in 1934. Also at that time its fog signal was discontinued. The light was removed from the tower and it was replaced with a red bell buoy that was established about 10 yards from the lighthouse in 50 feet of water.

The poor old station that had so often been battered by storms was now abandoned and left to the elements. A storm in 1946 caused such severe damage to the structure that the government dynamited the rest of it. Thus ended another one of America's historic maritime treasures, and the Avery Rock Lighthouse was lost forever.

This image shows Avery Rock Lighthouse in its prime. The image is rare since most photographs of the station were taken from the other side of the lighthouse with the bell tower, which was much more photogenic. In the early years, the lighthouse tender would supply the lighthouse with coal, only once per year. Regardless of how cold the weather got, the keepers needed to make the coal last. If they ran out, there would be no more deliveries.

Avery Rock Lighthouse with one of the several fog bell towers that occupied the site over the years. One time, during the tenure of lighthouse keeper Elson Small, in the early 1920s, he became extremely ill and delirious with fever. He was stricken just as a week-long storm hit the area. He was bedridden and unable to tend to his duties. Since there was no phone, his wife Connie had no way to call for help. While nursing her husband, Connie was required to maintain the light in the tower, keeping the lens lit and cleaned, as well as maintaining a constant fire in the boiler for heat. She was also required to keep the fog signal operating while caring for her husband. During this time she nearly collapsed from exhaustion, and toward the end of Elson's illness, Connie's vision became blurred and she was barely able to see. Fortunately, Elson eventually recovered.

Edward T. Spurling, wearing his lighthouse keeper's uniform, shown here with his wife, was the keeper at Avery Rock Lighthouse in the late 1800s. Prior to serving at Avery Rock Lighthouse he had been a keeper at Great Duck Island. After he left Avery Rock Lighthouse in 1899 he went on to become a lighthouse keeper at Franklin Island Lighthouse off the coast near Friendship from 1900 to 1911 and then on to Dice Head Lighthouse in Castine from 1911 to 1921. In 1999, his daughter Bea Spurling, then 95 years old, recalled that she spent her first eleven years of life living on Franklin Island and her parents didn't tell her much about life on Avery Rock, other than it was a hard life for her parents at that location.

When Elson and Connie Small were stationed at Avery Rock Lighthouse they did not have electricity. However, they did have a radio powered by batteries, but could only get one radio station. Connie Small soon found herself lonely and isolated at the lighthouse. Fortunately, the Lighthouse Service provided a library that would be exchanged every time the Lighthouse Tender would visit. In one of the libraries were two small booklets, "The Message," and "Deeds of Valor of the Coast Guard and the Lighthouse Men," written by the Rev. W. H. Law. Connie was so impressed by his writing that she wrote to him and for many years they corresponded with each other. Rev. Law encouraged Connie to correspond with other lighthouse keeper family members from all over the world, which she did for many years. Connie is shown here on the front steps at Avery Point Lighthouse in 1923.

This is a post card that was given to keeper Elson and Connie Small at Avery Rock Lighthouse from W. H. Law, who was widely known to lighthouse keepers throughout the nation as the "Sky Pilot to the Light Housemen." Law spent a lifetime on the high seas preaching the Gospel to lighthouse keepers and crews of lighthouse tenders. He also wrote stories about his experiences with them and kept in regular touch with hundreds of lighthouse keepers. Since there was no financial aid or pensions in those days provided to lighthouse keepers or their families, Law would personally financially help many of them. He also lobbied in Congress for higher pay for the light keepers. Connie and Elson were surprised and honored when one day a ship came to Avery Rock Lighthouse and on board to visit them was none other than Rev. Law. He also visited them in later years when they were stationed at Seguin Island Lighthouse off the coast of Bath, Maine.

Whenever her husband Elson would have to leave Avery Rock for supplies, Connie would be left alone on the island. Although she always had plenty of work to do around the lighthouse, sometimes she would just have a little fun and she said, "I'd get dressed up and really have no place to go."

This image shows how vulnerable Avery Rock Lighthouse was to storms. Often times waves and water would rush over the island, sometimes right into the keeper's house. During one storm the keeper sawed holes in the floor of the lighthouse so that the water would go into the basement. By doing so, he literally saved the structure from being washed away. Although nothing could be grown on Avery Rock, since there was no soil, this did not deter many of the lighthouse keepers. They would bring soil from the mainland and plant flowers, tomatoes, and even carrots in window boxes.

A three-day storm in 1926 nearly killed the keeper and caused the heavy damage shown here to the fog bell tower at Avery Rock Lighthouse.

Edwin Arthur Pettegrow arrived at Avery Rock Lighthouse to replace Elson and Connie Small who were transferred to Seguin Island Lighthouse. Pettegrow had a long and illustrious career in the Lighthouse Service and served as a keeper of numerous other Maine lighthouses, including Nash Island, Matinicus Rock, Petit Manan and Little River. He also served as a keeper at Isles of Shoals Lighthouse in New Hampshire. Often times his last name was spelled Pettigrew. Photograph courtesy of Eva Belanger.

Shown here, in his retirement years, is Avery Rock lighthouse keeper Vassar Lee Quimby with his wife, Lucy Florence Thompson Quimby. He arrived at Avery Rock Lighthouse in 1926. A devastating storm that hit Avery Rock Lighthouse that nearly destroyed the station, must have convinced Quimby that this was not a safe place to be stationed at and he soon requested a transfer. His request was granted and he was sent to Crabtree Ledge Lighthouse, a round caisson tower, but he didn't like that location either. While stationed there he sent a number of letters requesting a transfer. In one letter, he specifically requested a transfer to West Quoddy Head Lighthouse. Government paperwork in those days was no different than it is in modern times. After submitting a letter to the Department of Commerce with a list of lighthouses he would consider acceptable to be transferred to; the government wrote back to him saying they could not accept his letter because it was not submitted in duplicate and he was reprimanded for not doing so. At one point, he was offered the job of a watchman at the Little Diamond Island Lighthouse Buoy Depot in Portland. He did not accept it, because the job would require him to take a pay cut of 15% and he preferred to be a lighthouse keeper. Photograph courtesy of Gerald Quimby.

This painting of Maine's Boon Island Lighthouse was painted by lighthouse keeper Fred C. Batty who served at Two Bush Island Lighthouse and at Boon Island Lighthouse with Vassar Quimby. The painting was given to Quimby, who previously served at Avery Rock Lighthouse, as a remembrance of Quimby's time at Boon Island Lighthouse and their friendship. Interestingly, Batty's wife, Florence, grew up on Ram Island Lighthouse in Boothbay Harbor where her father was the lighthouse keeper.

Fred C. Batty also served at Saddleback Ledge Lighthouse. Batty's paintings were numerous and he painted many other lighthouses. One of his paintings is on display at the Seacoast Mission. The painting of Boon Island, shown here, has been in possession of the Quimby family almost since the day it was completed. It is now proudly hanging in a prominent place in the home of Gerald Quimby.

Vassar L. Quimby is shown here third from the left. The lighthouse keeper on the far left is Fred Batty and the man second from the left, may be retired veteran lighthouse keeper William C. Williams, both of Boon Island Lighthouse. The emblem on the hat of the unidentified man on the far right is not a Lighthouse Service emblem and may be that of the Steamboat Inspection Service or Bureau of Navigation.

Vassar L. Quimby may have been the only Maine keeper to be offered a transfer from Maine to the West Coast. On August 14, 1933, the Lighthouse Service offered him the job of 4th assistant keeper at St. George Reef Lighthouse in California. Although the pay was more, he must have thought the government officials had lost their minds by offering him a transfer to such a remote lighthouse, so far away from his home state. He turned them down flat. Quimby finally got fed up with the government bureaucracy and requested to be furloughed until he received a suitable transfer. On April 16,1933 the government granted him that request and he was furloughed. Eventually he was offered a position at Boon Island Lighthouse off the coast of York, Maine, a position that he accepted. It was here that he became a life long friend with lighthouse keeper Fred C. Batty.

Photograph courtesy of Gerald Quimby.

Libby Island Lighthouse

Entrance to Machias Bay — Machiasport, Maine

Rich in lighthouse history, the first lighthouse to be built on Libby Island dates back to 1817, when a small wooden tower was built. But, it was in 1823 that the young government of the United States erected a rubble-stone tower at Libby Island.

Apparently the 1823 tower had been very poorly constructed. It leaked, was damp, its mortar soon began to crumble, and the tower swayed in the wind, causing great anxiety for the keeper. Every time he climbed the tower he feared for his life. At one point the keeper propped boards up against the tower from various points to keep it from falling over. However, fall down, it did. Had the keeper been in the tower at the time, he likely would have lost his life or been seriously injured. The tower was rebuilt the following year.

Alexander Drisko is credited with saving the lives of sixteen men during a January gale during his last year as the keeper at Libby Island in 1891. With visibility nearly zero and the strong wind blowing the sound of the fog bell in the wrong direction, the schooner *Charles H. Boyton*, under the command of Capt. Elisha Allen, smashed on the rocks near the lighthouse. Three of the five dories on board the schooner were destroyed almost immediately, and the 16-man crew crowded into the two remaining dories. The men started to row to where they thought the island lighthouse was, but when they got close enough to the island, they could not find a safe place to land. They hollered and screamed for help. Exhausted and near the end of their strength, the crewmen saw a lantern being waved on the rocks. They followed the lantern around to the lea side of the island, where the winch from the station boathouse pulled them and their dories up the tramway and to safety.

James Jackman, one of the crewmen who was saved, later told a newspaper reporter in Machias, "Alex M. Drisko, the keeper of Libby Island was the man who saved us and good care we had afterwards." The men had lost everything in the shipwreck. Three of the crewmen were from Cutler and had no problem finding someone to take them home. However the other 13 men, having lost everything, appealed to the railroad for a train ride back to their homes in Gloucester, Massachusetts. The railroad company refused to help them. A stranger, hearing of their problem, paid their fare.

In the early years, Libby Island was a harsh place for a keeper to live, especially with no electricity, no phone, and only a rowboat as his lifeline to the outside world. As is typical of this area of "Downeast" Maine, the area has its share of fog. When a fog signal was installed at the station, it necessitated an additional keeper to be assigned to the station. Records in 1918 indicate that the fog signal sounded for 1,906 hours.

Philmore Wass in his book, *Lighthouse in My Life*, is credited with saving much of the history and stories of the island life and *Lighthouse Digest* magazine has recounted other stories of other families who lived there, too many unfortunately, to include in the pages of this book.

Sadly, the sounds of family life—the laughter, the sounds of children playing and the barks of the dog — have long disappeared from the Libby Island Light Station. Even the homes where the keepers and their families lived are now gone; the Coast Guard blew them up, leaving only faint memories in the dusty pages of time.

Owned by the U.S. Fish & Wildlife Service, Libby Island is now part of the Maine Coastal Islands National Wildlife Refuge and is off limits to the public during the nesting season. Where people once lived to help save the lives of those at sea, where keeper's raised their families, where children grew up learning the life of the sea, are all now gone and the only noise now is that of the birds. Yet, the tower at Libby Island still stands as a silent sentry from another era.

This early rare image shows the Libby Island lighthouse tower with what appears to be a 4th order lens in the tower, an older style bell tower and a dilapidated keeper's house. Look closely to the right of the tower and you will see the pile of rubble left over from when the previous tower collapsed. Two men are standing precariously on the edge of the outer walkway of the lantern room.

This image was probably taken around 1878 after a new lantern room was installed on the tower and a new fog signal building was built that housed a Daboll fog trumpet. The wooden bell tower is also a much better constructed tower than shown in the previous image.

John Grant, from 1850 to 1853, was the fourth lighthouse keeper to serve at Libby Island Lighthouse. When he later became keeper at Matinicus Rock Lighthouse, his son, Isaac Grant, served with him as an assistant keeper. Eventually, Isaac married Abbie Burgess who had gained worldwide notoriety for her heroic efforts at Mantinicus Rock Lighthouse, where her father had been the keeper prior to John Grant being appointed to the position.

Alexander M. Drisko (1836-1901) He served first as an assistant keeper in 1884 and then as head keeper at Libby Island from 1885 to 1891. He was not the first Drisko to be a lighthouse keeper here. Charles A. Drisko from 1877 to 1883, and William H. Drisko from 1883 to 1885 had preceded him as head keeper. When Alexander Drisko became the lighthouse keeper, his son-in-law Danford O. French was appointed assistant keeper. When Alexander Drisko retired from Libby Island, he still worked part time for the U.S. Lighthouse Service as a lamplighter to several minor aids to navigation, such as the spindle light at Moosabec Reach. Photograph courtesy of Chris Crowley.

This is the keeper's house on Libby Island in 1885. Barely visible, standing in the doorway, is Sophia Drisko; and Alexander Drisko, the keeper, is standing. Alice Drisko Newberry, their daughter, is shown sitting in the front. Next to her is Melissa Drisko French, daughter-in-law of assistant keeper Danford O. French, holding her son Frank French.

Sophia B. Drisko (1832-1927). She was the wife of Libby Island lighthouse keeper Alexander M. Drisko. At the time of her death she was the oldest person in Jonesport, Maine.

The original boat slip at Libby Island Lighthouse was quite a challenge for the keepers. At least five people are shown here trying to pull the station's heavy boat up the ramp and into the boathouse. Most of the injuries caused at lighthouses happened on the boat ramps.

Roscoe Johnson served as an assistant keeper at Libby Island Lighthouse from 1894 to 1896, then as head keeper at Little River Lighthouse from 1896 to 1898 and then as head keeper at Libby Island from 1898 to 1901. His son-in-law, Willie W. Corbett was also a light-

This image may be that of Assistant Libby Island Lighthouse keeper Danford O. French with his family. After being assistant keeper under Alexander Drisko, he became head keeper at Libby Island from 1891 to 1895. One morning after a severe storm in 1894, keeper French looked out into the water and saw a small piece of a shipwreck bobbing in the water with five men clinging for life on a chunk of wreckage. French immediately launched the station boat, and in fifteen foot swells, he went out and rescued the men, two at a time, with the last rescue taking place just seconds before the remains of the wreckage sunk.

house keeper and served at a number of Maine lighthouses, including Little River Lighthouse, where Johnson was once the keeper. The changes in stations all happened because in 1898, Frederic Morong, who was the keeper at Libby Island Lighthouse at that time, requested permission to trade positions with Johnson. It seems Morong wanted to be stationed at Little River Lighthouse so his children could attend the Cutler school. Having previously been stationed at Libby Island where he enjoyed life, Johnson was delighted with the offer and, Libby Island being a larger station, it provided Johnson with a higher rate of pay.

Albion T. Faulkingham served as a lighthouse keeper at Libby Island Lighthouse for 11 years in the early 1900s. He also served at a number of other Maine lighthouses. He is shown here on the right, with unidentified people at a 4th of July celebration in Eastport, Maine in 1925. Photograph courtesy of Lee Guptill.

Albion T. Faulkinham, a former keeper at Libby Island Lighthouse, is shown here in his retirement years in the early 1950s. The two gentlemen in the background are unidentified. Photograph courtesy of Lee Guptill.

Lighthouse keeper Charles Kenney and assistant keeper Harold Kilton at Libby Island in 1907. The island was great for farming and the keepers kept a wide variety of animals on the island, as is evident by this photograph. Photograph courtesy of Anita Romleski.

Libby Island Lighthouse keeper Charles Kenney is on the left with a small child and the assistant lighthouse keeper, Harold Kilton. Charles Kenney joined the Lighthouse Service as a crewman on a buoy tender in Portland and later served on a lighthouse tender. From there he took his first position as a light keeper at Petit Manan Lighthouse, until he was transferred to Libby Island in 1905. He remained there until 1912, when he transferred to Little River Lighthouse where he remained until 1923 when he was again transferred. This time to St. Croix Lighthouse, where he remained until his retirement in 1930. While stationed at Libby Island, he was credited with saving the life of Captain William J. Brenn from the wreck of the large schooner *Ella G. Ellis*, in which four of the crewmen lost their lives. Photograph, taken in 1907, courtesy of Anita Romleski.

This very early view of the keepers' homes and other out-buildings at Libby Island shows a harsh winter environment on the island. One can only imagine how cold it was the day this photo was taken. The small building to the left was the oil house.

This antique post card shows the beautiful keeper's house that once stood on Libby Island. The keeper is holding a small child and next to him is an assistant keeper with a child standing by him. Barely visible is the lighthouse dog, laying on the lawn. Family pets at lighthouses were quite common.

The families of lighthouse keepers Charles Kenney and Harold Kilton and perhaps a third lighthouse family on Libby Island Lighthouse around 1910-12. Photograph courtesy of Anita Romleski Herring.

Since everyone was dressed in warm clothes, it must have been a chilly day when this group photograph was taken at Libby Island Lighthouse circa 1911. Some of the people have been identified: (l-r) Fred Thompson, Della Marshall Thompson, Evelyn Cole Kenney, unidentified lady, unidentified lady, lighthouse keeper Charles Kenney, and Loring Thompson. The children in the front are Julian Kenney (l) and Ruth Kenney. Can you imagine working all day on a remote island wearing a long heavy dress? Photograph courtesy of Anita Romleski Herring; identification courtesy of Lois Sprague.

The fog signal whistle house as it appeared at Libby Island in the early 1900s when Charles Kenney was stationed there. Photograph courtesy of Anita Romleski Herring.

The telephone poles, shown in this photo from the early 1900s at Libby Island Lighthouse, are long gone, as are the two keeper's homes and barn shown here. Installation of telephone lines was the first time lighthouse keepers and family members were able to have instant contact with the outside world, something that dramatically changed their way of life. Photograph courtesy of Anita Romleski Herring.

The keepers' homes and all other buildings on Libby Island were kept in immaculate condition as shown here in this circa 1910 photograph. After automation, the houses were blown up.

Lighthouse Keeper's family gravestone at the cemetery in Buck's Harbor, Maine. Photo courtesy of Anita Romleski Herring who is the great granddaughter of lighthouse keeper Charles Kenney and granddaughter of lighthouse keeper Harold Kilton and daughter of Doris Sprague, who grew up at island lighthouses.

Everett A. Mitchell served as a keeper at Libby Island from 1922-1925. He is shown here with his son Everett A. Mitchell, Jr. Mitchell was one of three lighthouse keepers who lived on the island with their families. From Libby Island, he was transferred to Boon Island Lighthouse, Maine's tallest lighthouse, off the coast of York. In 1926 while serving as the principle keeper at Boon Island Lighthouse, his wife, a school teacher, convinced him that raising a family at such a desolate spot was not in their best interest and he left the Lighthouse Service. Photo courtesy of Winona Mitchell Dennison.

Lighthouse keeper Everett A. Mitchell sailing off Libby Island on an unusually calm day in 1922. Photograph courtesy of Winona Mitchell Dennison.

Lighthouse keeper Jasper Cheney on the boat ramp at Libby Island Lighthouse with his wife Tryphena, their son Roland and daughter Ella in the 1930s. Jasper Cheney served as the assistant keeper at Libby Island from 1933 to 1940 and as the head keeper from 1940-1949. Cheney joined the Coast Guard in 1928. He then joined the Lighthouse Service in 1931 and was first stationed at Rockland Breakwater Lighthouse. After Libby Island he served at Whitlock's Mill Lighthouse and retired from the Coast Guard in 1957. Also living at Libby Island Lighthouse with them was Forrest Spencer Cheney, who later also became a lighthouse keeper, as well as serving on the Nantucket Lightship.

Gleason W. Colbeth, is shown here wearing the white dress hat and the uniform of the United States Lighthouse Service. The man on the right is believed to be head keeper John Olson of Isles of Shoals Lighthouse, where Colbeth was stationed before arriving at Libby Island, where he served for over thirteen years. Although Colbeth joined the U.S. Lighthouse Service in 1930, he was already very familiar with lighthouses and had previously served in the Coast Guard as well as the U.S. Navy. His first assignments were as an "Additional Keeper," which was a position designated to someone who traveled from lighthouse to lighthouse to fill in when the full time keeper or assistant keeper at a light station went on vacation or was too ill to work. As an additional keeper, he served at Seguin Island Lighthouse under keeper Bracey. From there he went to Goose Rocks Lighthouse, then on to Ram Island and from there to Great Duck Island Light Station. His sixth station was at the Isles of Shoals Light in Portsmouth, New Hampshire, under John Olson and Wilbur Brewster, where he served eleven months. Finally he received a permanent appointment to Libby Island Lighthouse. Part of the thirteen and half years he served at Libby Island was under head keeper Herbert Wass, who was taken sick and never returned to the island. That left Colbeth in charge with assistant keeper Jasper Cheney. Eventually, Millard Urquhart was assigned as a keeper at Libby Island and the station now had three lighthouse families, "enough for a baseball team," he recalled.

During World War II, the Coast Guard assigned six young Coast Guardsmen to the station, whose primary job was to watch for enemy ships. Colbeth recalled that none of them were familiar with boats and, "Getting these young boys on and off the island for liberty was a major inconvenience for the lighthouse keepers."

One of lighthouse keeper Gleason Colbeth's sons, Julian, shown here with the family dog, Flash. Both loved to go duck hunting on the island. During one such expedition, he leaned his gun on a rock and Flash accidentally bumped the gun and it fell over. When the gun hit the ground, it discharged and the shot hit a muscle in Julian's right arm. Colbeth and keeper Cheney tried to patch him up as best they could and they radioed for help. He recalled in later years that Cheney was pretty good as a medic of sorts. It was four hours by the time the Coast Guard arrived to take him to the hospital in Machias, Maine. By that time he had lost quite a lot of blood. Although he recovered, he was never again able to use that arm to its fullest capability.

Libby Island Lighthouse in 1925 when Gleason Colbeth was stationed there. The long large building with the slanted roof between the two keeper's homes was the building that housed the cisterns. With three lighthouse keeper families living on the island, water was a valuable commodity.

Nearly every lighthouse had their share of family pets and many island light stations, such as Libby Island, were no different. Gleason W. Colbeth, who spent over thirteen years as a lighthouse keeper at Libby Island, is shown here by the bell tower at Little River Lighthouse with his dog "Flash" and his grandson Julian. The other woman in the photograph is not identified.

In his memoirs, Gleason recalled his memories of his dog "Flash," when he wrote the following . . . "The old saying is that 'A dog is man's best friend,' but I would rather put it this way – outside of God and the wife, God first, then the wife."

He continued, "My dog Flash was an Irish setter, pure bred, medium brown. She weighed about fifty pounds and was very intelligent – she could almost talk. Flash, I will say, was my true friend. She served with me at Libby Island light station for several years and when I was transferred to Little River Light Station, she went with me. She was always at my side and when I would go to the fog signal duties, she never got in front of me, as I trained her to stay behind me so that I would not step on her in the dark.

"My pal Flash also loved to go hunting. No matter how rough the sea was, at the crack of the gun, she was in the water to pick up the birds. Also, she picked up the wounded ones first, brought them ashore, laid them at my feet, and then went in after the dead ones. She loved to carry a bird home in her mouth, and was careful not to damage it.

"One day while serving at Libby Island Light Station, I went ashore for mail and supplies. Before I left the station I told Jasper Cheney, who was our second assistant keeper at the time, not to let Flash out of her quarters until I got ashore to Starboard, which was three miles distance.

"After I reached the mainland, I went home to Bucks Harbor by car, did my shopping and got my mail. I was home about three hours before returning to my boat. To my surprise, I found my old faithful friend in the boat waiting for her master. She was definitely tired out after the long swim and never again tried to follow me ashore, that is until I transferred to Little River Light Station in Cutler. Then she swam ashore several times, but the distance was only a quarter of a mile, a lot shorter than it had been at Libby Island.

"When I retired from my duties as the lighthouse keeper at Little River Light Station in July of 1950, my pal Flash retired with me."

Millard H. Urquhart, arrived at Libby Island Lighthouse after keeper Herbert Wass left the island due to illness. Urquhart had an illustrious career in the Lighthouse Service. Among other lighthouses at which he served, he was assistant keeper from 1928 to 1931 and the head keeper from 1931 to 1938 at Seguin Island Lighthouse.

Welton Colbeth spent many of his childhood years at lighthouses, such as Libby Island, where his father Gleason was the keeper, and throughout his adult life, he always had fond memories of those years. Welton shared a journal with the author of this book that was written by his father Gleason recounting his life from 1895 through 1977, much of it about life at the lighthouses.

Larson Alley, Jr. who, after returning from duty during the Vietnam conflict, served at a number of Maine lighthouses. Alley had followed in his father's footsteps and joined the United States Coast Guard. He served at the Fletchers Neck Life Boat Station before being offered the job as a relief lighthouse keeper. He served at Cape Neddick's "Nubble" Light, Goat Island Light in Cape Porpoise, Wood Island Light in Biddeford Pool, Cuckolds Light in Boothbay Harbor, and for six months was Officer in Charge at Libby Island Lighthouse.

While stationed at Cuckolds Lighthouse during a storm, he and the others stationed there, were ordered to evacuate. However, as waves rushed over the island, they could not safely reach the helicopter pad. As the storm worsened and the waves became larger, the water started to rise in the keeper's house. Alley and the others took refuge in the tower, an action which they believed saved their lives. In 1973, after serving over eleven years, Alley left the Coast Guard. Proud of his and his father's Coast Guard heritage, to this day he proudly displays a large Coast Guard flag from a flagpole at his home.

One of the last lighthouse pets to live on Libby Island was Gus, the station mascot, shown here, in February 1970. Photograph courtesy of David P. Bartholomay.

This 1943 photograph shows just how large the station at Libby Island was when Jasper Cheney was stationed there. As recorded in *Lighthouse Digest*, when Ella Cheney returned to Libby Island in the mid 1990s shock was mixed with nostalgia. In recalling the event in a story titled, "The Best Years of Their Lives," she said, "Our old swimming hole, the lighthouse and fog signal house are all the same as they were, but everything else was gone. I was told the other buildings had been burned. All the foundations had been filled in and grassed over. All the wooden planks were gone and even the boathouse. Just the slip was left. I felt so bad I cried."

In 2000, the Coast Guard did some back-breaking, hard work installing a new "wave–wall" at Libby Island Lighthouse. This is a wooden wall next to the landing slip that was built to protect the landing. Photograph by Lt. Christian Lund, USCG..

In 2000, the Coast Guard installed solar panels at Libby Island and removed some of the white paint from the tower to allow the bricks to breathe naturally. Today, it stands a silent sentinel from another era in time. Photograph by Lt. Christian Lund, USCG..

Little River Lighthouse

Cutler Harbor — Cutler, Maine

Located on a 15-acre island in the Bay of Fundy at the entrance to Cutler Harbor in Cutler, Maine, the Little River Lighthouse Station was established in 1847. The current tower here was built in 1876 to replace an earlier tower and the current keeper's house was built in 1888. The first boathouse, built in 1847, was replaced by the current structure in 1887. In 1905 a granite block oil house was built using some of the original stone that had been left on the island from the first keeper's house and tower that had previously been demolished.

For 130 years Little River Lighthouse station was occupied first by families of the keepers of the United States Lighthouse Service and then in 1939 by Coast Guard keepers. The end came in a letter dated December 23, 1974 when E. D. Schederer, Chief of Staff for the United States Coast Guard announced that Little River Lighthouse would be discontinued as a manned and staffed light station. This did not come as a surprise to most people, because on September 19 of that year the Coast Guard had started advertising for a caretaker for the island.

After the Coast Guard left the island, caretakers maintained the property for a time under lease agreements from the Coast Guard in cooperation with the University of Maine and the Cutler Naval Air Station before it was finally abandoned and left to the elements to decay and rot away.

On March 2, 1979 the Coast Guard convened a Board of Survey for the purpose of removing and razing Little River Lighthouse. In 1981 the Coast Guard informed the Cutler Association that all the buildings on the island, including the tower, would be leveled, and the island would be put up for sale. Jasper C. Cates, Jr., one of Cutler's town fathers, wrote strong letters of protest to various government officials, which eventually convinced the government bureaucrats to change their minds.

As part of the Maine Lights Program that concluded in 1998, Little River Lighthouse was offered up for adoption to any government, community or nonprofit agency. At the conclusion of the program in 1998, nearly three-dozen Maine lighthouses were transferred to new owners. However, no one wanted ownership of Little River Lighthouse, including the National Park Service, U.S. Fish & Wildlife Service, The State of Maine or the local community. They all cited various reasons for not wanting the lighthouse with statements that it would be too expensive to restore, or it would be impossible to save and restore. Other reasons cited were that it was too remote, the insurance would be too expensive, and others felt that it was the federal government's responsibility to save it.

Since no one came forward to adopt the lighthouse and the lighthouse continued to deteriorate from neglect and the elements, in 1998, Maine Preservation declared Little River Lighthouse as one of Maine's Ten Most Endangered Historic Properties.

In April 2000 the lighthouse was licensed by the Coast Guard to the American Lighthouse Foundation, of which I was president at that time. Almost immediately the American Lighthouse Foundation began to work with the Coast Guard to have the light returned to the tower. After extensive work to restore the lantern room, the Coast Guard installed a modern optic in the tower.

Having worked so hard to get the lighthouse relit, I was extremely determined to ensure the future of the historic station. When the light station was declared excess property, I spent several weeks preparing the application for ownership of the lighthouse for the American Lighthouse Foundation. And on July 27, 2002, in ceremonies held in Cutler, the lighthouse became the first one in New England and the third lighthouse in the nation to have its ownership transferred under the National Historic Lighthouse Preservation Act of 2000. Later, the American Lighthouse Foundation received a special award from the National Trust for Historic Preservation for being part of the pilot program of that federal law.

For the next seven years volunteers worked to raise money and restore the light station. In 2007 a local group, The Friends of Little River Lighthouse, was formed as a chapter of the American Lighthouse Foundation for the ongoing restoration and long term care of the lighthouse.

In February of 1847, the Committee on Commerce of the House of Representatives of the United States approved $5,000 for the construction of Little River Lighthouse. The brick tower, painted white, was attached to a keeper's house made of granite blocks. This design was a near twin to the Prospect Harbor Lighthouse in Prospect Harbor, Maine that was built a couple of years later. Notice the primitive barn and fenced area. The lighthouse keepers had to be somewhat self-sufficient to keep their families fed and they kept many animals on the island such as cows, pigs and chickens. The first lighthouse keeper was Elijah Shiverick who served until 1853. Other keepers who lived in this house were John McGuire from 1853 to 1865, Oliver Ackley from 1865 to 1866 and Edward Noyes from 1866 to 1870.

Maine's Prospect Harbor Lighthouse, as shown here in 1850, was a near twin to the first Little River Lighthouse Station. The structure no longer stands and has been replaced by the lighthouse that still stands today.

Lighthouses of the Sunrise County

Lucius Davis became the lighthouse keeper at Little River Lighthouse in 1870. He must have liked the island life at the lighthouse as he stayed there with his family for an amazing 26 years until 1896. He had only been there for seven years when, in 1876, the government decided to build a new tower at the lighthouse to house a new Fresnel lens that had been imported from France. The lantern room from the old tower was removed and the top was capped and the old tower became part of the living quarters. It must have been an exciting time for lighthouse keeper Davis. The station had a new barn, new fencing and other improvements were made.

In 1886 a book written by Mary Bradford Crowninshield titled, *All Among the Lighthouses or The Cruise of the Goldenrod,* was published. The book was a historical fictional account of a cruise that she and her brother took to visit Maine's lighthouse on board a lighthouse tender. Her uncle, who was the lighthouse inspector for the First District of the United States Lighthouse Service, had invited them along. Although the book is a true account of the trip it was fictionalized with name changes and stories that were based on her memories. In fact, the real name of the lighthouse tender that she took the voyage on was the Lighthouse Tender *Iris*. There were many artist engravings of the lighthouses that she visited in the book and with the exception of this image of Little River Lighthouse, most were fairly accurate depictions of the lighthouses.

Although the granite keeper's house was fairly spacious, it was always damp, difficult to heat and with time the windows and the roof leaked. In an area plagued by fog and heavy blowing rainstorms, this eventually caused great stress to lighthouse keeper Lucius Davis and his family. By 1888, Davis saw the improvements he was really waiting for. The old granite keeper's house was demolished and new home was built. During the construction time it is unclear where the keeper and his family lived. They might have camped on the island or boarded on the mainland. Although this house still stands today, it has been altered several times over the years. At this time the tower was painted red to allow it also to be used as an easily seen day-mark from the water. This photo, taken shortly after construction, still shows a lot of building debris and even granite blocks from the old house strewn about. It is unclear what the platform shown on the left was for. However, look closely, and you'll see the keeper's cow standing amongst the debris.

This is a vintage view of Little River Lighthouse Station approaching the house from what is now a wooden walkway leading from the boathouse over the island to the house. In those days there was only a footpath. Cleary shown are the barn, the pyramid bell tower and a chicken coop.

The lighthouse tender sits anchored in Cutler Harbor during the construction
of the second keeper's house in 1888. Notice all the logs stacked on the beach.

Photograph of Little River Lighthouse from the water
taken from a lighthouse tender as it approached the island.

This vintage photograph is unique because of the unusual angle from which it was taken, giving the station a different appearance. The caged-in area next to the barn was most likely for chickens. Barely visible is a tin advertising sign on the barn for laundry soap, an extremely unusual item to see displayed at a light station.

Frederic William Morong (1842-1920) was the keeper at Little River Lighthouse from 1898 to 1910. He joined the Lighthouse Service in 1890 at the age of 47, and served at a number of other Maine lighthouses including Petit Manan, Libby Island, and Lubec Channel lighthouses. Morong was married twice and fathered eleven children. He fathered five children with his first wife Mary Jane Brawn who died in 1876. In 1878 he married Sarah Jane Cooke and they had six children. Before becoming a lighthouse keeper, he had spent most of his life on the sea, first as a seaman, then a mate, and later a master. He operated steamships along the coast of Maine and New Brunswick. Two of his sons joined the Lighthouse Service. His son, Alonzo, went on to become a keeper at Goose Rocks Light in 1905, Petit Manan from 1906 to 1909, Cape Elizabeth (Two Lights) for eight years and at Browns Head Lighthouse for thirteen years. Interestingly Alonzo's son, Clifton who was born at Cape Elizabeth Lighthouse, eventually also became a lighthouse keeper.

Another son of Frederic William Morong, Frederic Morong Jr., joined the Lighthouse Service in 1922 and became a district machinist and worked his way up to Lighthouse Inspector. Well-liked by the lighthouse keepers, he gained national prominence for his famous poem, "Brassworks."

Frederic William Morong, Sr. retired from the lighthouse service in 1915 and settled in Lubec where he died in 1920.

Lighthouse keeper Frederic W. Morong is shown at Little River Lighthouse on this vintage post card. An amusing anecdote of Morong's time at the lighthouse is told about one of his daughter Myra's suitors. It seems that after the young man had rowed across the harbor from Cutler, the weather got up and the harbor became very choppy and the Morongs thought it might not be safe from him to return to the mainland, so they invited him to spend the night on the island. At one point he excused himself. After a while they missed him and worried about him, but finally located him walking up from shore with a bundle under his arms. He had rowed back to the village for his pajamas.

A number of Maine's lighthouse keepers gathered at Little River Lighthouse in the late 1800s when this photo was taken by Libby Island Lighthouse keeper Danford French. Lighthouse keepers and their families often traveled to visit other keepers for holidays, generally on the 4th of July. A number of the keepers and wives got in the photo. One man can be seen leaning out of an upstairs bedroom window. A lighthouse keeper posed on the outside walkway of the lantern room looking through a telescope. Little River Lighthouse could be called a light of many colors. When the second tower was first built, it was painted white. When the new keeper's house was built, it was painted red. This was done so that it could more easily be seen in the fog and snowstorms. However, in 1880, the lighthouse inspector wrote that the red tower should be painted white. For some reason, instead of painting the tower white, it was painted dark brown. In 1900 the inspector again wrote that the tower should be painted white and that contractors need not be hired to do the job, as it was the keeper's responsibility to paint the tower.

The first boathouse at Little River Lighthouse. The small dory on the boat ramp that was rowed by hand was the keeper's only lifeline to the mainland for supplies and emergencies. Before electricity, the boat had to pulled up the boat ramp by a hand winch. Built in 1847, the boathouse was torn down and replaced in 1881 by the boathouse that stands there today.

Two women posing on the back porch of Little River Lighthouse. The overhang area at one time was a totally open porch that was added after the keeper's house was built. At some point three quarters of it was closed in to make a pantry, which in later years became the radio room, and today it is a bathroom.

This 1920 hand-painted image by M. Richards was given as a gift to Doris Kilton Sprague, granddaughter of lighthouse keeper Charles A. Kenney, so that she could remember her happy times at Little River Lighthouse.

Machiasport native Charles A. Kenney was the lighthouse keeper at Little River Lighthouse from 1912 to 1921. He is shown here in approximately 1917 with (l-r) his mother, Mrs. Small, his daughter Marcia Kenney who married Harold Kilton who also became a lighthouse keeper, and Marcia's daughter Doris Kilton (Sprague) then age 12.

Kenney joined the Lighthouse Service in 1902 and served on a buoy tender in Portland and then on the Portland Light Vessel (lightship) before being transferred to Petit Manan Lighthouse in 1902. In 1905 he was sent to Libby

Island. After Little River he was sent to St. Croix River Lighthouse where he retired in 1930 at the age of 70. Doris Kilton (Sprague) spent 11 years of her childhood summers with her grandparents at Little River Lighthouse and recalled in later years that she loved every minute of it. On her first visit to the island she climbed over the fenced-in area to walk to the boathouse. Suddenly a cow came from nowhere and took a slight jump at her, and for the remainder of that first summer on the island she never left the fenced-in area again. She later learned that the cow was quite harmless. She followed her grandfather everywhere and even learned how to operate the fog bell, which was her favorite volunteer job. Photograph courtesy of Anita A. Romleski.

A rare photo of the kerosene lamp that once lighted the Fresnel lens in the tower at Little River Lighthouse in the days before electricity.

Since very view photos were ever taken of the mechanism that once turned the Fresnel lens in towers, this photo at Little River Lighthouse is considered rare.

Lighthouse keeper Charles A. Kenney by the bell tower at Little River Lighthouse. The two ladies are unknown, however the little girl is Doris Kilton (Sprague). Photograph courtesy Anita A. Romleski.

Willie W. Corbett is shown here in his younger years playing the violin. As well as entertaining his family, he often left the island to play on the mainland and often traveled to nearby Cross Island Life Saving Station to play with some of the crewmembers stationed there. Photograph courtesy of Delia Farris.

Willie W. Corbett as a young 26-year old man when he joined the U.S. Lighthouse Service in 1908. The number "2" on his jacket indicated he was a second assistant keeper. He came to Little River Lighthouse as the head lighthouse keeper in 1921 after having been previously stationed at Saddleback Ledge, Monhegan, and Tenants Harbor lighthouses. Because the U.S. Lighthouse Service was dissolved in 1939, he was the last U.S. Lighthouse Service keeper to serve at Little River Lighthouse. However, he continued to serve as the keeper, even after the Coast Guard took over, until he retired in 1945. Photograph courtesy of Neil and Allie Corbett.

Willie and Velma Corbett with their eight children at Little River Lighthouse. It's hard to imagine raising such a large family like this in the small keeper's house that did not have electricity. However, they all pitched in to help while enjoying a variety of games that were played inside as well as outside. Photograph courtesy of Neil and Allie Corbett.

This is one of the cows that were kept by the Corbett family at Little River Lighthouse. Although there was a small amount of hay growing on the island at the time, hay for the cows was supplied by Willie Corbett's brother-in-law Pilsbury Dinsmore. When the hay was harvested on the mainland, it was hand-stuffed into burlap bags and then brought to the island, all of which was quite a project. While stationed at Tenants Harbor Lighthouse, Corbett had a cow that produced a plentiful supply of good milk, so he took the cow with him to Little River Lighthouse when he was transferred there. The cow got seasick on the boat ride and never again produced a plentiful supply of milk. Another cow did not like island life, and kept swimming to the mainland, so keeper Corbett had to go and fetch him and bring him back to the island. After a few times doing this, Corbett gave up and the cow spent its remaining years on the mainland.

Neil Corbett, son of keeper Willie Corbett, recalled in all the years that he lived on the island, he never once used a flashlight at night and he learned to walk everywhere in the dark. Returning home one dark night, he was unexpectedly startled as right in front of him in the dark was the cow. In his thick Downeast Maine accent he recalled, "Boy, that took a jump on me - took a jump on her too!"

He recalled another cow that the family had that was standing on the edge of the rocks eating moss when she slipped and fell and hit her head on the rocks and died instantly. "Yup, she was a nice cow, too. Boy oh boy, she tasted plenty good the next day too." Photograph courtesy of Gordon Corbett.

Family life on an island lighthouse had its ups and downs, just like family life anywhere. Little River Lighthouse keeper Willie Corbett holding his son Lester who, sadly died at nine years of age. Photograph courtesy of Neil and Allie Corbett.

As the daughter of veteran lighthouse keeper Roscoe Johnson, Velma Johnson Corbett, wife of Willie W. Corbett, was familiar with lighthouse life long before she married a lighthouse keeper. She is shown here with son Myron Corbett who was born on Maine's remote Saddleback Ledge Lighthouse Station where they were once stationed. Photograph courtesy of Neil and Allie Corbett.

The community of Cutler as it appeared in 1932 when Willie W. Corbett was the keeper at Little River Lighthouse. Although there have been some changes, the community looks basically the same today.

Over the years many of the lighthouse keepers of Little River Lighthouse and their descendants, who have remained in the area, have attended the Cutler United Methodist Church, shown here in this circa 1930 photograph. In 2000 the American Lighthouse Foundation held its first meeting with the community in the church basement to introduce themselves to the townspeople. In 2001 during the land-based part of the relighting ceremony of Little River Lighthouse, spotlights lighted the outside of the church for the first time in its history. The gathering for the relighting ceremony was reportedly the largest gathering in the town's history.

Neil Corbett in his U.S. Army uniform is shown here with his mother Velma. Neil spent the first 18 years of his life growing up at island light-houses. Neil Corbett was no fan of island life and as a young man used every chance he could to get off the island. When Neil left the island to join the Army, his father rowed him to shore. At that time he looked his father straight in the eye and, as he shook his Dad's hand, he said, "Island life may have been good enough for you but it's not for me and when I come back, I'll never set foot on that island again." His father looked back at him and said, "That's okay, I understand." When Neil did come back from the Army he settled in Cutler, raised a family, and ran a successful lobster business. He was also active in baseball, which was big in Maine at that time. He was a player and later a coach and did some umpiring. In 2002, at the age of 85, Neil Corbett was inducted into Maine's Baseball Hall of Fame.

Perhaps Neil inherited his love for baseball from his dad, Willie Corbett. In 1918, Willie Corbett paid $1.00 to take the ferry from Rockland, Maine to Boston, MA, and then paid 50 cents to get in to see the last game of the 1918 World Series. That was a lot of money in those days, considering lighthouse keepers were not highly paid. But it was worth it. Willie Corbett witnessed history, when New England's hometown team, the Boston Red Sox, won the World Series.

It wasn't until 2006 at the request of lighthouse restoration volunteer, Hal Biering that Neil finally returned to the island and the lighthouse where he had grown up. In fact he made several trips out to the island in 2006 and the following year. Photograph courtesy of Neil and Allie Corbett.

The lighthouse keepers at Little River Lighthouse had telephone service many years before electricity arrived at the island. Although this primitive system was upgraded in later years, when a telephone line finally reached the island for the first time, it immediately opened up the outside world to the keepers. Nearly every evening the keepers communicated over the phone line with the keeper at Libby Island Lighthouse. Myron Corbett, son of lighthouse keeper Willie W. Corbett, wrote in later years, "In those days one used those old wall style telephones with considerable awe and distrust, speaking into the mouthpiece and staying right there to hear, as the cord was too short to allow much movement. You would take the receiver off the hook and listen to see if the line was clear, then replace it and ring other parties on your line, or ring one for the central office. Way back then if you had to call Cross Island Life Boat Station you asked for 41 RING 4 or 41 RING 3 for Libby Island Light. They would RING 2 for Little River Light." The telephone also brought comfort to many families in town waiting for an overdue lobster boat. There were no radios in those days. They would call the lighthouse keeper, who in turn would call back to the mainland when he saw the vessel approaching the island and advise the families on shore that the boat was safely on its way back home.

This vintage view of the basement of the keeper's house at Little River shows a heavy cast iron coal-burning boiler that was used to heat the house. It is no longer there and bits of pieces of it were strewn about the island when the Coast Guard removed it.

The 4th order Fresnel lens that was once in the tower at Little River Lighthouse as it appeared on August 15, 1960. It was a fixed lens with two revolving flash panels, which were weight driven. This lens mysteriously disappeared when it was removed from the tower.

This nice image of Little River Light Station clearly shows the architecturally beautiful pyramid bell tower that was first put into operation on Sept. 30, 1871. Myron Corbett, son of lighthouse keeper Willie Corbett, recalled that as well as for its intended purpose, his mother also felt it was a good place for violin lessons. Myron said it was also a great place for the kids to kick back and do some whittling, a tradition that very few kids today even know how to do.

To operate the fog bell, the lighthouse keeper inserted a big crank into the machinery to raise the weights to the top of the tower and, except for emergencies; this was all the care it took, plus a little oiling now and then. However, when the machinery broke, the duty of ringing the fog bell usually fell to one of the keeper's children, if they were old enough. Myron Corbett wrote, "The tools needed were a stopwatch, kerosene lantern and maybe a couple of short length matches or toothpicks to prop your eyes open." His brother Neil recalled in later years that he spent many a cold night shivering for hours in the unheated bell tower ringing the bell by hand. The logbook at Little River in 1947 recorded the most continuous fog recorded at the station as 525 hours. However, Neil Corbett said the problem with those records were that no one ever bothered to check with the old records from the time he was living there when his father recorded 542 hours of continuous fog.

Many times, while huddled up in the fog bell tower and ringing the bell by hand, all one could hear was the heavy roar of the surf. On really stormy nights, waves would hit the tower. On those nights, if the bell was being rung by hand, whichever lighthouse kid was in the tower would be too scared to accidentally doze off. One of those big Nor'easters did in fact knock the bell tower off its foundation. Rather than attempt to save and restore the tower, the Coast Guard, in its infinite wisdom, decided to simply burn the structure to the ground and replace it with a modern cast iron bell holder - and a valuable slice of the station's architectural beauty was destroyed forever.

Myron Corbett wrote shortly thereafter, "For those families – the Davis's, the Morongs, the Johnsons, the Kenneys and the Corbetts – whose tour of duty in the old Lighthouse Service included this station, the bell tower will always be in their memories, along with the lumber-laden coasting schooner beating her way into the harbor in the teeth of a northerly, or drifting eastward, while headed westward, with wind scarier than hen's teeth."

This close-up view of the lantern room shows the small brass lighthouses that were once on each stanchion of the lantern room railing. The whereabouts of all them are unknown to this day. When the station was automated, souvenir hunters removed them. However, there are a few lighthouses around New England where these small brass lighthouses still remain, such as Cape Neddick, "Nubble" Lighthouse in York, Maine and Nobska Lighthouse in Woods Hole, Massachusetts.

Notice also the drapes that were hung in the lantern room and closed during the daylight hours to protect the priceless Fresnel lens from the sun's harmful rays.

Myron Corbett is shown here as a youngster at Little River Lighthouse. Little River Lighthouse was a family station and at a family station everyone helped out. Such was the case when it was time for Myron's father, lighthouse keeper Willie W. Corbett, to take his annual vacation. That particular year his vacation time was for the deer-hunting season. As Myron recalled later in life, his father was as near tired of island life as he had ever been in his 35 years of being a lighthouse keeper. Unfortunately, the government had no substitute lighthouse keeper to fill in for Corbett, who then wrote the government with a number of reasons why his 14-year old son could serve as the substitute keeper. The government replied saying that if he so chose to follow this path, if anything went wrong at the lighthouse while his 14-year old son was left in charge, it would cost Corbett his job, plus the government would not under any circumstances pay a 14 year child for the position as a substitute or relief keeper.

Willie Corbett was not to be deterred and went on vacation. He was confident that his son and other family members would take good and proper care of the lighthouse while he was gone.

After his return, he wrote the government officials and told them what a competent job his 14-year-old son had done to take care of the light station during his absence. A few weeks later a letter arrived addressed to Myron Corbett. Upon opening it and to his complete surprise enclosed was a government check made out to him. He wrote years later, "At that point in my life, that represented a shocking bit of money. All $45.00 of it was quite well in excess of my wages of 25 cents an hour cutting cod tongues and cheeks at Dennis's Fish Wharf."

Photograph courtesy of Gordon Corbett.

Velma and Willie Corbett in their retirement. They raised eight children at a number of Maine lighthouses. Little River Lighthouse was their last station. Velma was no stranger to lighthouses when she married Willie Corbett. She was the daughter of Roscoe Johnson who served at a number of Maine lighthouses including Little River Lighthouse. Velma Johnson spent more time on Little River Island Lighthouse than any person in history. In 1939 when the Lighthouse Service was merged with the Coast Guard, Willie Corbett, as with other keepers, was given the opportunity to stay on as a civilian keeper or join the Coast Guard. He joined the Coast Guard and was given the rank of Boatswain Mate First Class. He retired on August 1, 1944. Photograph courtesy of Delia Farris.

After the pyramid bell tower at Little River was destroyed, the bell was mounted on this steel platform with an automatic striker. When the bell was discontinued, members of the community moved it to the mainland where it is now on display in Cutler's Bell Circle.

Aerial view of Little River Light Station showing the barn and bell tower that were later destroyed. In this image a telephone pole is barely visible. Also shown here is a dormer that protruded from the upstairs bathroom. It is no longer there. Payson K. Tucker, who was the lighthouse keeper at that time, wrote an interesting account in January of 1948 of a fox that swam to the island, "A big red fox walked to our front porch this past fall, no doubt searching for our two, newly acquired kittens, namely 'Tommy' and 'Skipper.' The fox met with a shooting accident prior to intervening with the kittens, hence they are still intact." Tucker had it better than the previous keepers. He didn't have to row back and forth to the mainland. The government gave him an 18-foot motor dinghy.

When CWO Kenneth Black, (1923-2007), USCG, was the Office In Charge of Group Quoddy Head, he made an inspection trip to Little River Lighthouse and was shocked at what he saw. He said he felt as though he had stepped back in time when he saw a light station that was still operating without electricity. Dave Hardman, who was in the Coast Guard from 1954 to 1964, was stationed at Little River Lighthouse in 1957-1958. Hardman recalled in later years that at that time the station had a gas powered water pump and the light from the tower was still lit with a kerosene (IOV) lamp. Hardman wrote that a one cylinder Fairbanks Morse gas powered pump, which had to be hand cranked whenever water was needed, supplied the domestic water. At that time the Coast Guard keepers were using a Briggs and Stratton powered washing machine and they ran the exhaust hose out of the window. Black ordered that the station be electrified at once. After electrical wiring was installed, a one lung Witte diesel generator was used, until an underwater electric cable could be laid from the mainland to the island.

A lighthouse keeper's work is never done, as is evident from this image showing the work that needed to be done to strip off the old paint and repaint the house at Little River Lighthouse. All the work needed to be done by the lighthouse keeper, who at this time was Gleason W. Colbeth, who is shown here holding his grandson, Julian. The Coast Guard offered him no help in painting the house, saying it was all part of his one-man lighthouse job. Notice the clothes on the line and the fact that the barn was still standing when this photo was taken. Photograph courtesy of Welton Colbeth.

After being stationed at Libby Island for over thirteen years, Gleason W. Colbeth came to Little River Lighthouse in 1945 to replace veteran lighthouse keeper Willie Corbett. Colbeth was no stranger to Little River Lighthouse; he had served here once before, many years earlier as a temporary keeper for two weeks when Willie Corbett took a vacation. He recalled in his written memoirs that Little River Lighthouse was the perfect family station and a great spot where one could be his own boss.

He recalled how the government gave him a new twenty-foot boat with a new engine. Every day in season he brought his children to the mainland for school and picked them up in the afternoon. His son Hollis attended Washington Academy and son Welton went to the Cutler grammar school.

Like the Corbetts and other keepers before him, he maintained a garden and had a number of farm animals. His wife Lillian L. (Beal) learned how to operate the fog bell. In later years he bragged about his wife and their many years of happy marriage. He was also extremely proud of the fact that they were good Christians and raised their children as good Christians.

Little River Lighthouse keeper Gleason W. Colbeth takes a moment off his work to pose for this photo with his grandson Julian. A Navy veteran of World War I, Colbeth served duty on the battleship North Carolina. He had also served a stint in the Coast Guard as a surfman at Cross Island Life Boat Station before joining the Lighthouse Service. Colbeth had several accidents during his lighthouse career; the most serious happened when he was stationed at Isles of Shoals Lighthouse in New Hampshire where he injured his back. His back problem got more serious as time went on, but he wasn't one to complain and he loved his job as a keeper at Little River and he said he loved the friendly people in Cutler.

When the Lighthouse Service was dissolved in 1939, he chose to go into the Coast Guard rather than remain as a civilian lighthouse keeper, a decision that he would later regret. When the Coast Guard Commanding Officer made an inspection trip to Little River Lighthouse, he realized that Colbeth was slowing down and suggested that he take early retirement because of his medical problems. Colbeth had heard from other lighthouse keepers that the Coast Guard was squeezing out the old lighthouse keepers in favor of younger Coast Guardsmen. He told his commanding officer that he was happy with his job at Little River and content there; besides, he could not afford to retire. He still had two boys at home. He asked if his medical problems showed any indication of his not being able to perform his duties and the officer said no and said he would give him a good report. As he dropped him back on the mainland in Cutler, the commanding officer was very cordial to him and gave no indication that there would be any changes.

However, a short time later he received a letter saying that, "I was to report to the retirement board in Boston," which in turn sent him to Coast Guard doctors for a physical. A short time later he was given his disability discharge papers and told to vacate Little River Lighthouse at once. He said they told him rather coldly, "to go find another job." He was given disability pay of $109.35 per month.

And so, in July of 1950, Gleason Colbeth ended his career as a lighthouse keeper. So much for being a good employee for so many years; the Coast Guard had a different way of doing things than the old Lighthouse Service did. But he did not hold any hard feelings; he was too much of a good Christian for that. He then bought himself a new boat and started to do some lobstering and hired out his boat for fishing parties. Photograph courtesy of Welton Colbeth.

Little River Lighthouse Station looked very pristine after keeper Gleason W. Colbeth gave the keeper's house a fresh coat of paint in the 1940s. Look closely and see the clothes on the line as they dry in the fresh breezes off the ocean. Photograph courtesy of Welton Colbeth.

This is the lens that replaced the Fresnel lens in the tower at Little River Lighthouse. However, it was removed from the tower in the 1975 and replaced with a modern optic atop a skeleton pole at the edge of the island near where the old fog bell once stood. The whereabouts of this lens is unknown. As with the Fresnel lens that was once in the tower before this lens, it also mysteriously disappeared, lost in the paperwork of time.

When the last light was removed from the tower at Little River in 1975, it was replaced by this optic, mounted atop an erector style skeleton tower at the edge of the island. Also at that time the fog bell was replaced with the modern foghorn shown at the base of the skeleton tower. This structure remained as the light for Little River until 2001, when, after being dark for 26 years, the Coast Guard installed a modern optic in the tower after volunteers of the American Lighthouse Foundation restored it. Unfortunately, when the skeleton tower was discontinued, rather than save it as an historical artifact, it was removed from the island for disposal.

Robert Ray Cale, Sr. (1929-1967) holding his daughter Sharon Jean Cale, in front of the tower at Little River Lighthouse. Sharon was born in February 1953. By the time Cale arrived at Little River Lighthouse in the mid 1950s, he was a veteran Coast Guardsman and lighthouse keeper, having served previously around the country as well as at Southwest Harbor and the Quoddy Head Coast Guard Stations. His first lighthouse duty was at Libby Island Light Station where he served from August 1949 through January 1951 and from there he was stationed at Cross Island Life Boat Station before coming to Little River Lighthouse. Cale retired from the Coast Guard in 1956.

In honor of his father, former Little River lighthouse keeper, Robert Cale, Sr., his son, Robert Cale Jr. and his wife Elaine, were married at the Cross Island Life Boat Station where his father had once been stationed. They are shown here on the steps of the old Coast Guard Station on Cross Island on their wedding day, July 24, 1995. Photograph courtesy of Elaine and Robert Cale, Jr.

Sadly, the old United States Life-Saving Service building on Cross Island is no longer standing. It was replaced by a newer building, which was also eventually abandoned by the Coast Guard. Over the years, the lighthouse keepers from nearby lighthouses and the surfmen from the life saving station became well acquainted with each other. Shown here are Georgia Snell and Jeannie Snell Chellis.

The keeper's house at Little River Lighthouse (1954-1955) as it appeared during the time that Robert Ray Cale, Sr. was stationed there. Although the roof appears to need some work at that time, the station looks relatively the same today. Photograph courtesy of Elaine and Robert Cale, Jr.

BMC Russell W. Reilly, USCG, is shown here with his father Paul Reilly. After an illustrious career in the United States Navy (1948-1952) and the United States Coast Guard (1955-1971), Reilly finished his career in 1971 as a keeper at Little River Lighthouse, where he had also previously served as a keeper from 1956 to 1960. He had also served at a number of other Maine lighthouses in the Sunrise County, including, Libby Island, West Quoddy, Petit Manan and Whitlock's Mill. He served at Little River Lighthouse with fellow Coast Guardsman Dave Hardman.

The keeper's house was still heated with coal at that time, which was delivered by the Coast Guard Buoy Tender *Laurel*. The coal was in 50-pound burlap bags, which he and the other keeper had to bring across the island in wheelbarrows and then dumped into the basement of the house, the same way it had been done since the station was established in 1847. During this time the Coast Guard keepers served 19 days on duty and then got five days off. The keepers had three dogs on the island named Louie, Punk, and Blub. A reporter for the *Bangor Daily News* who visited the island at that time said the dogs loved their island paradise.

By the time Reilly returned to Little River for his second tour of duty on the island and his last assignment before retiring in the 1970s the station had been automated and an oil-burning furnace had replaced the coal-burning furnace. Photograph courtesy of Kelly Reilly.

As a young Coast Guardsman, Burleigh Chandler was stationed at Little River Lighthouse from 1964 to 1967. He is shown here giving his daughter, Brenda Lee, a ride in the station's wheelbarrow. During his stint in the Coast Guard Chandler also served as a keeper at Bear Island and Petit Manan lighthouses.

Donna Chandler, wife of Coast Guard keeper Burleigh Chandler, climbed atop the fog bell at Little River to pose for this photograph in 1965. Although it was a three-man station at this time, family members often came out to visit.

By the time this photograph was taken of Little River Lighthouse, the barn that once housed the animals of the lighthouse keepers had been removed. The walkway at that time had a railing to assist the keepers in getting to the fog bell in inclement weather.

As a young Coast Guardsman, Terry Rowden, from Michigan, shown here in a 1966 photograph, came to Little River Lighthouse in a transfer swap with another Coast Guardsman. Rowden had been notified that he was being sent to West Quoddy Lighthouse in Lubec. At the same time another Coast Guardsman had received orders that he was being sent to Little River Lighthouse in Cutler. The other Coastie complained to Rowden that he had just bought a sports car and did not want to be stationed on an island. He asked if Rowden would mind switching assignments with him. Rowden agreed and was sent to Little River Lighthouse. However, the other Coast Guardsman's orders were soon changed and he was shipped to Vietnam.

Terry Rowden often comments on how the trading of assignments changed his life. While stationed at Little River Lighthouse from 1968 to 1970, he met and married Cynthia Cates, a local Cutler girl and they stayed in Cutler where they raised their family.

In later years Terry Rowden helped with the restoration of the lighthouse and in 2007, his wife, Cynthia Rowden, became an officer of the Friends of Little River Lighthouse.

As a young Coast Guardsman, David P. Bartholomy arrived at Little River Lighthouse in 1970. He has previously served on the USCG Buoy Tender *Cowslip* at the Boothbay Harbor Search & Rescue Station, and he had served as a relief lighthouse keeper at Burnt Island Lighthouse and Cuckolds Lighthouse. Before coming to Little River, he served at nearby Libby Island Light Station. Although he recalled loving Libby Island as much as Little River, he said that "compared to Libby Island, being stationed at Little River was like paradise."

The unannounced visits by tourists to the remote island often offered the Coast Guardsmen as much entertainment to them as they did in return. Bartholomy recalled, "Early one morning, while running to answer the telephone in just my underwear, I had forgotten that the beautiful island often attracted unexpected tourists, regardless of the time of day. Upon answering the telephone, I turned to look out the window and discovered two women looking in the office window. I am not certain who was more surprised, the women, the person on the other end of the phone, the other keeper on duty, or me, as I let out a yell of surprise. Thankfully, because of a lack of fresh water, I had not been showering when the phone rang!"

The farm animals were long gone from the station by that time, but the lighthouse did have a Beagle named Freckles as its mascot. Bartholomy wrote many years later, "Truly it is a shame that wonderful experiences are often wasted on youth. Little did I realize then, the history of the light station or that the days of manned lighthouses would soon end."

John A. Arrington (l) was the Coast Guard Officer In Charge from March 1972 to 1973 and served at the station with Albert Vachon and Gary Sill. On the right is Anthony W. Weyer who replaced Al Vachon in 1973. Little River Lighthouse was a three-man stag station at that time. Photograph by Albert Vachon.

Seaman Gary Sill, USCG, served at Little River Lighthouse in the early 1970s with Al Vachon and John Arrington when the lighthouse was a three man station. Sill, who was from Ohio, is shown here with the small wooden boat with a 9-hp Johnson outboard that took the crew back and forth between the mainland and island. Photograph by Albert Vachon.

Little River Lighthouse Station as it appeared on a tranquil, but bitterly cold, winter day in the winter of 1972. Notice the TV antenna attached to the top of the tower. Photograph by Albert Vachon.

The abandoned Little River Lighthouse shows the tower rusting away. The old telephone poles were still standing and had not been used in years.

Ruth Corbett Farris, daughter of lighthouse keeper Willie W. Corbett, is shown here rowing near the site of the old Steamboat Wharf to Little River Lighthouse. She lived on the island until she was 24 years old. When she married local lobsterman Glenn Farris, she settled on the mainland and from her home near the waterfront she always had the island in her view until the day she died.

For 34 years she wrote a column for a local newspaper that chronicled a cherished way of life that has disappeared from the American scene. Ruth's husband bought this dory for $10.00 from the Coast Guard at an auction and Ruth literally made hundreds of trips to the island rowing in this boat.

In the 1990s Ruth rowed out to the island with Donna Morong, a descendant of Little River Lighthouse keeper Frederic Morong. Donna later recalled that trip and wrote how disgusted they both were by the way the light station had been left and abandoned by the Coast Guard and how Ruth always prayed that someone or some group would step forward to save the lighthouse. Her prayers were eventually answered; however she died before she could see that happen.

The people of the community dearly loved Ruth, who was affectionately known locally as "Mother Nature." After her death, a memorial stone was placed in the town's Bell Circle near where the fog bell from Little River Lighthouse is now on display. Photograph courtesy of Ruth Leubecker.

In April 2000, volunteers from the New England Lighthouse Foundation, d/b/a the American Lighthouse Foundation, under the direction of the author, made their first site inspection to the island and the lighthouse to assess the situation. Shown here are members of that team: (l-r) Jeremy D'Entremont, Douglas Bingham, Timothy Harrison, Kenneth Black and William Collette, Jr. Also present was Kathleen Finnegan, who took the photo. What they found was a rusted and leaky tower, a keeper's house in shambles, a rotted walkway, downed trees, and tons of debris on the island.

Many years prior, Little River Lighthouse had been under Ken Black's command when he was Officer In Charge of Group Quoddy Head. He recalled his first visit to Little River many years previously and said he recalled that it was like stepping back in time. He said he was amazed when he found the lighthouse never had electricity, even up to those modern times. He immediately ordered that electricity be brought to the island.

On the visit this day in 2000, Black said he was not shocked by the deteriorated condition of the station, although even he admitted that it was worse than he had expected. He remembered when the station was in pristine condition.

When the volunteers of the American Lighthouse Foundation made their first inspection trip to start the assessment as to amount and scope of work that would need to be done at the lighthouse, the first person they met was Neil Corbett who grew up on the island as the son of lighthouse keeper Willie Corbett. Neil is shown here talking with Ken Black, who founded the lighthouse museum in Rockland, Maine. Ken was known in lighthouse circles as "Mr. Lighthouse."

Although Neil and Ken hadn't seen each other for many years, they knew each other from many years previous when Ken had been Officer In Charge of Group Quoddy Head. On that first meeting, Corbett recounted many stories to the volunteers and did so subsequently over the next few years. Relying on his memory, which was always sharp, he acted as a consultant for the restoration of the lighthouse.

On our first visit to Little River Lighthouse in April of 2000, Ken Black and I posed for this photo by the Little River Lighthouse fog bell, which is now on display in the Cutler town circle. The bell is inscribed 1896 with the words U.S. Lighthouse Establishment.

Thanks to the efforts of Jasper Cates, Jr., on March 21, 1971 United States Senator Margaret Chase Smith (the first woman to serve in both houses of Congress and the first woman in history to have her name placed in nomination for President of the United States) secured the 1,677-pound fog bell for the community. However, getting the bell to the mainland would take a lot of brute force and displaying it would cost money.

Nearly two years later the bell was still not on display and in a letter to the town of Cutler, dated January 15, 1973, the government told the town that if the bell was not put on display as promised the government would authorize its removal to Rockland for display at the lighthouse museum.

The town won that battle.

On the first visit by volunteers of the American Lighthouse Foundation to the island in April 2000, they found that over 60 trees had fallen over the wooden walkway that was rotted out so badly that it was nearly impossible to walk on. At that time the badly deteriorated boathouse was slipping into the ocean and most of the boat ramp had been destroyed.

A corner of the kitchen in the keeper's house as it appeared in April 2000. The rest of the house was in much worse shape.

The oil house at Little River Lighthouse is shown as it appeared in April 2000. Having been built from the original granite blocks from the first keeper's house and tower, it is the most historically significant structure on the island.

The historic relighting of Little River Lighthouse on October 2, 2001 was a two-part ceremony. The first part took place at dusk on the ocean with an armada of over 30 boats, including a Coast Guard vessel. The second part of the ceremony took place on the mainland at Cutler's Bell Circle. Originally known as the "The Village Green," the "Cutler Bell Circle" was dedicated during the 1974 July 4th ceremonies. During the dedication ceremony, Ruth Corbett Farris, daughter of lighthouse keeper Willie Corbett, sang the national anthem and at the ceremony, Jasper C. Cates, Jr., the town's betterment leader, appropriately named the old fog bell the "Bell of Peace." However, it was not until 1980 that a monument was approved for mounting the bell.

Little could Jasper Cates, Jr., have realized in 1974 that many years later, after the terrorist attack of 911, another ceremony of peace would be held at Bell Circle when on October 2, 2001 the re-lighted Little River Lighthouse would be declared a Beacon of Freedom to the World.

The relighting ceremony of Little River Lighthouse was reportedly the largest gathering in the town's history. As part of that ceremony, two wreaths were laid at the bell, one honoring the memory of those who lost their lives in the terrorist attacks of 911, and the other in memory of the lighthouse keepers who served at Little River Lighthouse.

After having been dark for 26 years, thanks to the joint efforts of the American Lighthouse Foundation and the United States Coast Guard, this modern optic was placed in the tower and it was relit on October 2, 2001.

As president of the American Lighthouse Foundation from 1992 through 2007, the author led the effort to save Little River Lighthouse. The History Channel produced a "Save Our History" segment on Little River Lighthouse and here I am being interviewed by the film crew in October 2001, the day before the lighthouse was relit. The next seven years were spent working on the restoration, as well as raising money for the restoration. In 2007, volunteer Hal Biering and Tim Harrison became co-chairmen of the newly formed Friends of Little River Lighthouse, a chapter of the American Lighthouse Foundation.

A Coast Guard helicopter visits Little River Lighthouse on October 1, 2001, a day before the lighthouse was to be relit after having been dark for 26 years. The flag was draped from the lighthouse in preparation for the ceremony on October 2, when the lighthouse was relit as a "Beacon of Freedom to the World," in memory of the lighthouse keepers and family members who served at the lighthouse and in memory of those who lost their lives in the terrorist attacks a few weeks earlier on September 11.

Three of the children of lighthouse keeper Willie Corbett pose with a replica of Little River Lighthouse at the relighting ceremony in October of 2001. They are (l-r) Kathleen Corbett Johnson, Florence Corbett Armstrong and Purcell Corbett. They all had fond memories of life on the island. The model of the lighthouse was built by Donald Perkins and was later put on display at the elementary school.

In a large ceremony held at Bell Circle in Cutler on July 27, 2002, ownership of the Little River Lighthouse was transferred from the United States Coast Guard to the nonprofit American Lighthouse Foundation.

Presenting the ceremonial gold key of the lighthouse to Tim Harrison (r), president of the American Lighthouse Foundation, was Kenneth "Sam" Hill, Chief, USCG Aids To Navigation, Southwest Harbor (l) and Commander Hank Haynes, Commander, USCG Group Southwest Harbor.

During the ceremony that transferred ownership of Little River Lighthouse, the official flag of the Secretary of the United States Department of Commerce, which features a lighthouse, was displayed above the fog bell that was once used at Little River Lighthouse. It is the only official flag of a federal agency that has a lighthouse on it. At one time the United States Coast Guard operated under the authority of the Department of Commerce. The Coast Guard is now part of the Department of Homeland Security.

Local residents Jean Bergeron and Jasper Cates, Jr. sang, "Let the Lower Lights Be Burning," at the Transfer of Ownership Ceremony for Little River Lighthouse on July 27, 2002. At this time, ownership of the lighthouse and the entire island were transferred to the New England Lighthouse Foundation, which was then doing business as the American Lighthouse Foundation.

Several hundred people attended the Transfer of Ownership Ceremony for Little River Lighthouse on July 27, 2002. Some of the dignitaries who officiated in the ceremony led by the author, were Rev. Betty Palmer of the Cutler United Methodist Church; Maine State Legislator Representative Martha Bagley; Commander Hank Haynes, USCG Commander Group Southwest Harbor; P. Dan Smith, Special Assistant to the Director of the National Park Service in Washington DC; and Saundra Robbins, Project Manager of the General Services Administration. The presentation of the colors was provided by the United Veterans Honor Guard of Washington County and music was provided by the River City Salon Orchestra and the Blue Hills Brass Quintet. At the ceremony, the New England Lighthouse Lovers (NELL) made a cash donation to the restoration of the lighthouse. Local resident Cynthia Cates Rowden coordinated events for the ceremony.

On January 9, 2004 a television crew from Bill Green's Maine visited the island with volunteers. On that day the temperature was minus 20 degrees and the wind chill, with gusts, was 40 to 60 degrees below zero. Although the sky is clear in this image, it wasn't too long afterward that the winds picked up and storm moved in. Removing the television crew and volunteers from the island was a feat later written about in local papers as "The Frightful Trip to Little River." By the end of the trip, the cameras had frozen, but the film that was captured of the sea smoke made the national news on the following day.

Lighthouses of the Sunrise County

Restoring the keeper's house at Little River Lighthouse was a project that took eight years, requiring countless hours of work by many volunteers and contractors that cost nearly a quarter of a million dollars. However restoration continues to be an ongoing project.

Volunteers from the American Lighthouse Foundation, the United States Coast Guard, and even some Boy Scouts, helped in painting the tower at Little River Lighthouse in September 2006. This was not an easy project. Towers like this generally require repainting every three to four years.

Volunteers painting the lantern room in September 2006. On top of the ladder is Bob Trapani, Jr., Executive Director of the American Lighthouse Foundation. To his right at the highest point is volunteer Al Vachon who served as a keeper at the lighthouse in the early 1970s.

On September 3, 2006, Neil Corbett, who grew up at Little River Lighthouse, made a return visit to the lighthouse to attend the first ever community church service held on the island by the Cutler United Methodist Church. The service was officiated by Pastor David Arruda. Afterwards, Neil recounted memories of his life at the lighthouse to many of those in attendance. The date of the first church service on the island was significant as it was also the birthday of Willie C. Corbett, the last keeper of the United States Lighthouse Service to serve at the lighthouse, and it was the birthday of Timothy Harrison, who led the effort to first lease the lighthouse, then get ownership of it, and finally the effort to restore and save the lighthouse.

Volunteer Hal "Mr. Hal" Biering on the newly painted spiral staircase inside the tower at Little River Lighthouse. Bob Trapani, Jr., Executive Director of the American Lighthouse Foundation and his wife Ann, spent several weekends bringing the stairs back to their original red color in 2006. Painting underneath the stairs and the under part of the floor of the watch room was a dangerous project and extremely difficult to accomplish. Photograph by Chessie Johnson.

Hal Biering, known locally and affectionately as "Mr. Hal," with Neil Corbett on the island at Little River Lighthouse on September 3, 2006. Neil Corbett was one of the children of lighthouse keeper Willie Corbett. "Mr. Hal" started coming to Cutler from Alabama in 2003 to help restore the lighthouse and has come every summer since. His daughter read about the efforts of Tim Harrison and the American Lighthouse Foundation in Parade Magazine and told him that he might consider helping out. He had previously spent some summers in Canada restoring lighthouses. He called Harrison, and within a few weeks "Mr. Hal" arrived in his motor home in Maine.

Hal, a retired consulting engineer, is also a jack of all trades, who brought his own tools and could make, design, build, fix and restore just about anything. Most days, he took the small motorboat out to the island by himself, bringing supplies and working alone. Volunteers showed up to help him from time to time. Often times, if the group didn't have money for certain supplies, "Mr. Hal" paid for them himself. On his second year he returned with his friend Betty who traveled out to the lighthouse with him nearly every day to help. She must have liked what she was doing and enjoyed "Mr. Hal's" company, as they were married shortly after that.

"Mr. Hal" became so popular that TV stations, newspapers, and magazines came out to interview him and write about him. When TV reporter Amy Sinclair of CBS-TV 13 asked him how much he charged for his services, "Mr. Hal," replied, "I do this for free. I don't play golf, I don't play bridge, I just like to work and help. Someday, people will be able to say, 'A man from Alabama came to Maine each year to help save this lighthouse'."

"Mr. Hal" piloting the small boat on one of over 1,000 trips he made back and forth to the island and Little River Lighthouse to work on the restoration.

Former Little River Lighthouse Coast Guard keeper Al Vachon and Hal Biering ("Mr. Hal") in 2005 at the lighthouse. This was the first time in 32 years that Vachon had been back to the lighthouse and he returned to spend his vacation time helping to work on the restoration. He had such a good time that his wife Pat returned with him in following years to help.

Vachon said he was amazed at the deterioration that had taken place since he was stationed there in 1972-73. He commented that the town of Cutler looked almost the same as it did when he left and the people were just as friendly now as they were then.

Vachon was stationed at the lighthouse with Engineman John Arrington and Seaman Gary Sill. In those days they had two pet cats named Tom and Stubbs. They also had a pet raccoon that somehow had got stranded on the island.

Vachon recalled that during his stay on the island the biggest excitement was taking the boat to town and waiting for the mail truck to arrive. That experience must have had an impact on him, because after he left the Coast Guard he became a rural mail carrier for the next 31 years.

The second community church service held by the Cutler United Methodist Church on the island at the end of the summer in 2007 drew over 100 people. Lacking a full time pastor the church service was officiated by Tim Harrison. The service opened appropriately with the singing of the hymn "Shall We Gather at the River." Ruth Farris played a portable keyboard and former Little River Lighthouse keeper Terry Rowden provided the sound system. Those in attendance sang a variety of songs including, "This Little Light of Mine, I'm Going to Let it Shine" and the official theme song of the American Lighthouse Foundation "Legend of the Lighthouse," written by volunteer Judi Kearney.

Descendants of Little River Lighthouse keeper Willie W. Corbett gathered for a group photo on the island in August 2007.

Although the restoration of the Little River Lighthouse is still an ongoing project and the station will also require high maintenance, in 2008 it was made available for overnight stays. Fees from the overnight stays will help defray the cost of maintenance, while allowing people to experience, in some small way, what living at a lighthouse was once like.

Lubec Channel Lighthouse

Lubec, Maine

Built in 1890 the Lubec Channel Lighthouse is seen by every person crossing the International Bridge to or from Campobello Island, Canada and Lubec, Maine in the United States.

Although the lighthouse was built as a stag station, the lighthouse keeper's wives or other family members would often visit. This was against the rules, since getting on and off the lighthouse was considered too dangerous for visitors. Connie Small, whose husband, Elson, was the keeper here from 1920 to 1922, recalled when she was visiting her husband they saw the lighthouse tender approaching the lighthouse. Fearing that the lighthouse inspector might be on board, she went and hid in the basement. However, realizing that she would be found during an inspection she decided to return to the living quarters and take whatever scolding might be given. Fortunately, the lighthouse tender did not stop and went on past the lighthouse.

Fred Morong Sr. was the first lighthouse keeper to serve at Lubec Channel Lighthouse and he later served at other lighthouses in the area including Little River Lighthouse.

The first floor of the lighthouse housed the living room and the kitchen, which was recalled in later years as being quite cozy. When Connie Small first visited the lighthouse she was amazed by how nicely everything fit in a round room. She said she would recall years later, her uncle Loring Myers, the Head Keeper at the lighthouse, sitting in his rocking chair, as he would admire the view across the bay. Another floor held a bedroom and above that was the lantern room deck. The basement held a cistern for water, a coal bin, oil tanks and wood, which was sometimes used in addition to coal for the stove.

Lighthouse keeper Loring Myers, who was on duty here from 1890 to 1923, an amazing 33 years, probably held the longest tenure at the lighthouse. In later years he commented that he must have walked on the deck around the lighthouse at least 50,000 times.

In 1939, when a passing steamer did not receive the normal greeting from the lighthouse keeper they stopped to investigate. Nathan Alley, an assistant keeper at the lighthouse was found unconscious, having been overcome by fumes from the stove. Although he was taken to land for medical treatment he soon died. The lighthouse was automated after that and its keepers were removed.

Although the Coast Guard would make occasional visits to the lighthouse over the years to check on the automated beacon, the structure, without any general maintenance, began to deteriorate badly. Also, ice floes had caused the tower to begin to tilt and there was some worry that it might fall over. At that point the Coast Guard decided it would discontinue the lighthouse and even discussed the possibility of tearing it down. However, a campaign by the community was started to save the lighthouse. Known as "Save the Sparkplug," the group handed out automobile sparkplugs to help gain attention while they conducted a lobbying campaign.

Finally, by 1992, $700,000 had been appropriated to save the lighthouse and in 1993 its foundation was stabilized and the lighthouse was saved. A few years later the tower was given a fresh coat of paint and other maintenance was done to the lighthouse.

When the government decided that it no longer wanted to own lighthouses, the Lubec Channel Lighthouse was offered up for adoption, free of charge to any nonprofit or other government agency that might want it. Although some interest was expressed, all felt that the lighthouse would be too expensive to maintain. Finally the government put the lighthouse up for auction to the highest bidder and in September of 2007 it was sold to businessman Gary Zaremba, president of Artisan Restoration Group of New York City for $46,000.

Lubec Channel Lighthouse
as it appeared in 1931.

Frederic W. Morong (1842-1920) He joined the U.S. Lighthouse Establishment in 1890. In 1899 he become the first lighthouse keeper to serve at the newly constructed Lubec Channel Lighthouse. Later Morong went on to serve as a keeper at Libby Island, Petit Manan and Little River Lighthouse. He retired from the Lighthouse Service in 1915.

Loring William Myers, shown here in his lighthouse keeper uniform, served as the keeper of the Lubec Channel Lighthouse for an amazing 33 years. However, as well as being a lighthouse keeper, Myers pursued many other business interests. He was a merchant, real estate agent, owned a sardine plant and several smoke houses and he was an ingenious inventor. It was his meticulous record keeping and lobbying that eventually helped convince Congress to dredge the channel. Like many people in life Myers had his ups and downs in life. His first wife and three of his four children died of diphtheria on Grand Manan Island before he became a lighthouse keeper. The fourth child went to live with him in Lubec where he married Abbie with whom he had additional children with. When he retired he continued to stay busy and he loved to garden and tend to his apple orchards. Photograph courtesy Dorothy Pickard, granddaughter of Loring W. Myers.

Being a lighthouse keeper in a round lighthouse completely surrounded by water, gave lighthouse keeper Loring Myers a lot of spare time to invent a number of items. He was most proud of the lifeboat that he invented and is shown here standing in it while a friend was rowing. Standard lifeboats, with which ocean liners were equipped, hung from davits. Many times, while a ship was listing during sinking, the boats would tip, throwing the people into the sea. Myers' invention would permit the people to board the lifeboat, which would remain on the deck of the sinking ship, and then simply float off as the larger vessel sank beneath the surface, thus saving the lives of the passengers. Many experienced sea captains who saw the lifeboat hailed it as revolutionary and the government even approved it. However, Myers was never able to secure the necessary financing and the big steamship lines of the time opted for cheaper and less effective lifeboats. Myers often commented that more lives would have been saved on the Titanic if they had his lifeboat on board.

A scale model of the Myers Lifeboat that Myers made to before he actually built one of his lifeboats.

Although the artist is unknown, the Myers family is proud of this pen and ink drawing of him. Myers spent many years as a captain of a steamer that ran between Boston and Yarmouth, Nova Scotia before taking on the position of assistant lighthouse keeper under Fred Morong at the Lubec Channel Lighthouse. He eventually became the Head Keeper. Over the years he was credited with a number of rescues of small boaters and some took refuge in the tower until they could safely reach shore.

It was not uncommon in the days of lighthouse keeper Loring Myers for ladies from Lubec to take a boat out for a Sunday sail. One group however, nearly lost their lives in the currents of the dangerous water around the lighthouse. Myers saved them and after they took refuge in the lighthouse he eventually got them all safely back to shore.

Constance "Connie" Scovill and Elson Small, on their wedding day in 1920. Elson became the assistant lighthouse keeper at Lubec Channel Lighthouse on November 1, 1920 and the couple were married a few days later on November 23. He later became the head keeper.

Connie Small enjoyed drawing and painting. She sketched this image of her husband, Elson, who was the keeper at Lubec Channel Lighthouse. He later served as the keeper at St. Croix River Lighthouse, Avery Rock Lighthouse, Seguin Island Lighthouse, Portsmouth Harbor Lighthouse and others.

Although Connie Small would often go out to the Lubec Channel Lighthouse to visit her husband, they maintained a home on the mainland in Lubec. Connie is shown here with other family members on the mainland with the family dog. "Joe."

Although the water is calm in this photo, this was not the norm at Lubec Channel Lighthouse. One false move and a fall into the fast moving icy currents by the lighthouse could mean death. When Connie Small first visited the lighthouse in 1920 she was nearly too scared to jump from the boat and grab the rungs of the ladder and make the climb up. Her husband assured her it would be okay that he'd be right behind her and to always look up and never look down. Connie said in later years that those words always stayed with her and she lived her life by them.

Connie Small is waving at the photographer as she holds on to the ladder at Lubec Channel Lighthouse in 1921. Above her on the ladder is her cousin Emma Davis.

Connie Small (l) with her cousin Emma Davis on the lower outer deck in 1921 at Lubec Channel Lighthouse.

Large passenger steamships like the "Camden," shown here, owned by the Eastern Steamship Company, often made regular visits to Downeast, Maine. It was large vessels such as this that necessitated the building of lighthouses. The "Camden" is shown here on a visit to Lubec. When rail service became popular, ships like this disappeared from the scene. By 1948 the Eastern Steamship Company sailed its last passenger steamship.

The fog bell at Lubec Channel Lighthouse, shown here in this close up photograph, was removed and given to the Lubec Historical Society in 1978. When the bell was brought to shore there was a parade and ceremony dedicating the bell at its new location on the grounds of the historical society, where it remains to this day, a forgotten relic of the past.

This modern optic now serves as the beacon inside the lantern room at Lubec Channel Lighthouse. It replaced a rare 4th order Fresnel lens.

One of the Coast Guard crew who painted the lighthouse in 1993, takes a moment to pose for a photograph on the outer lower deck of the freshly painted lighthouse.

In 2007, at the age of 82, Mr. Everett Melvin Cross recalled when he was hired in 1951 by the government to help do some maintenance work on the Lubec Channel Lighthouse. Part of the work was to install metal rings around the base of the lighthouse. Cross was placed in a bosun's chair and lowered down to perform the work, which was completed in two days. In 2000 he wrote the following:

The Channel Lighthouse

Traveling down South Lubec Road
To Visit West Quoddy Head Light,
Look eastward and you will see,
A man made structure,
Of black and white.

Some say it looks like a Spark Plug,
I know it as
The Channel Light.

Many years it stood there,
Thru turbulent storms and rising tides,
To warn the seaman of the rocks and sand bars,
As they slowly pass by.

Silently the grayness of the fog creeps in,
You will hear a mournful sound,
And on top of the lighthouse,
The Beacon light goes slowly round and round.

I pray it stay forever,
Somehow I think it will
And that it will be maintained,
'Till time stands still.

Lubec Channel Lighthouse as it appears today. Barely noticeable is the fact that the tower tilts about three degrees.

Moose Peak Lighthouse

Mistake Island — Near Jonesport, Maine

Like many other American lighthouses, very little remains today of what was once a glorious lighthouse station on Mistake Island near Jonesport, Maine.

The first lighthouse station here was established 1826 on what has been recorded as one of the foggiest sections of the Maine coast. Because of this, a fog signal building was erected in 1912 that housed the steam machinery for a powerful diaphragm fog signal. From 1914 to 1934 the keepers here recorded an average of over 1,600 hours of fog per year. Records indicate that in one year, the fog signal sounded continuously for 181 straight hours.

In 1851 the original Moose Peak lighthouse tower was demolished and a new tower was built. In 1888 the lighthouse was refitted for a gigantic second order Fresnel lens. In the early 1900s the original keeper's house was demolished and a new one was built.

For many years the station was the home to lighthouse keepers and their families. Holidays were celebrated, visitors came, and the sound of work and play could be heard from the island and the house.

In a 1996 interview, the late Dana Pearson recalled the days when her father, Capt. James Anderson, was a keeper at a number of Maine lighthouses, including Moose Peak Lighthouse where he was assigned in 1907. She said she spent the first six years of her life on the island until her father temporarily bought a house on the mainland so she could easily attend school. She didn't recall too much about life at Moose Peak, but her mother told her that it wasn't much different than the other island lighthouses they lived on in later years. She recalled, "It was the only life we knew, and we enjoyed it. We did whatever nature would let us do. We didn't have to come ashore to be entertained, because we could entertain ourselves." With a slight smile, she also remembered that they never had to lock the doors, saying, "I never knew what a house key was!"

The end of the Moose Peak Lighthouse came in 1972 when the station was automated. The keeper's house was offered up for sale, but even though a buyer was found, EPA standards, rules, and regulations made the sale financially impractical. So the Coast Guard sought permission to destroy the house. The Maine State Historic Preservation Office gave its permission, saying that the 1903 house didn't have any historical significance, a decision that would not hold weight today.

In 1982 a military unit conducted a training exercise to blow up the keeper's house. The demolition didn't go exactly as planned. Although the explosion destroyed the keeper's house, it also damaged the helicopter-landing pad and broke panes in the windows of the lighthouse tower. Unfortunately, no one has ever shared photographs of the demolition and cameras surely would have been on hand for a training exercise. What could have been so secret as to not share photos with historians, even to this day? Regardless, a vital part of Maine's lighthouse history was destroyed forever and never given a real chance to be saved for future generations.

Today, Mistake Island is managed by the Maine Chapter of the Nature Conservancy, as part of the Great Wass Island Preserve. The lighthouse is still maintained by the Coast Guard and operates on solar power.

The earliest known image of Moose Peak Lighthouse Station. Since there were a number of people in the photograph, including some people in the tower, there may have been a work crew on the island at the time.

This image shows the long covered walkway that the keepers used. This was a great benefit in times of inclement weather or fog, when it might have otherwise been impossible to get from the keeper's house to the tower.

Moose Peak Light, Maine.

A vintage post card showing the new watch room and lantern that were installed in the Moose Peak Lighthouse. The new lens was lighted on September 5, 1888. This gave the light station an entirely different appearance.

The fog signal building at Moose Peak Lighthouse was built in 1912. Look closely and you will see chickens grazing on the ground. Nearly every island lighthouse station had chickens as a source of fresh eggs and meat. The foghorn can be seen protruding from the building.

This image shows the Hornsby Akroy engines, air tank, and other mechanisms that were once needed to operate the foghorns at Moose Peak Lighthouse.

With a white fence around much of the Moose Peak Lighthouse, this image almost gives the appearance of a tranquil farm-like setting. The fence not only kept the small children of the lighthouse keepers from wandering too far, but it kept the animals close at hand. This photograph was taken prior to 1903, before the house, shown here, was demolished and a much larger keeper's house was built.

Albion T. Faulkingham was a lighthouse keeper at Moose Peak Lighthouse. Prior to Moose Peak Lighthouse, he had served for 11 years at Libby Island Lighthouse. Having also served at Whitehead Lighthouse from 1905 to 1909, he later served as a keeper at Matinicus Rock and Owls Head lighthouses and ended his career at the Prospect Harbor Lighthouse, where he served from 1935 to 1939. He is shown here with his wife Lucy, and daughters Marcha, Florence and Beatrice (Dee Dee).

In a 1992 interview Beatrice recalled that island lighthouse was often lonely. The girls watched for their father's boat to return from the mainland with supplies, wondering what presents he would bring them, as he always did. Knowing the girls were lonely, keeper Faulkingham often came back with a new pet for them, usually a dog or a cat. When the children were of school age, they were sent to the mainland to live with their paternal grandparents while attending school. During this time they missed their mother.

When an underwater phone line was installed, the girls spent many hours on the phone with their mother. Weather permitting, they would sometimes go back to the island for weekend visits and, of course, they spent the summer months at the island lighthouses. Photograph courtesy of Vicki Tuthill, daughter of Florence Faulkingham.

Beatrice Faulkingham, daughter of lighthouse keeper Albion Faulkingham, is shown here later in life. As a young lady, she met William (Willie) Henry Woodward. However, since she was living on an island lighthouse station, most of their courtship was via telephone. When she married Woodward at age 20, little did she realize that he would eventually join the Coast Guard and also become a lighthouse keeper, just like her father had been.

As a lighthouse keeper's wife, Beatrice, following in her mother's footsteps, went where her husband went, and spent four years at the Isles of Shoals Lighthouse in New Hampshire, which she said were the worst four years of her life. The water there was rough more than it was calm and the lighthouse seemed to be in the path of every storm that hit New England.

They were eventually transferred back to Maine and to the Manana Island Fog Signal Station near Monhegan Island where they were stationed from 1928 to 1934. Beatrice said this was her favorite of all the places they ever lived. They were later transferred to Monhegan Island Lighthouse and from there to the Doubling Point Range Lights on the Kennebec River. They finished their career at Two Lights at Cape Elizabeth when Willie Woodward retired. The couple then moved back to Jonesport, Maine to operate a deep sea fishing business. Photograph courtesy of Jean Gupthill.

Although William (Willie) Henry Woodward never served at any of the lighthouses in Washington County; his photo is worthy of inclusion here because he married Beatrice Faulkingham, daughter of Libby Island and Moose Peak Lighthouse keeper Albion Faulkingham. Beatrice and William lived at a number of Maine lighthouses. While they were stationed at the Doubling Point Range Lights on the Kennebec River, tragedy struck their family. Their ten-year old daughter, Lucy Mae, while playing in the water by the lighthouse, lost her life. It was believed at the time that the little girl suffered a heart attack while in the water, which led to her drowning. Photograph courtesy of Jean Guptil.

Joseph Muise served as a lighthouse keeper on the Maine coast for many years, first with the U.S. Lighthouse Service and then with the Coast Guard when it took over the Lighthouse Service in 1939. It was his brother-in-law, also a lighthouse keeper, who convinced him to join the Lighthouse Service. Married to Annie Seavey, they raised six children during his lighthouse keeping years. His first station was Moose Peak Lighthouse. From there he went to Mt. Desert Lighthouse and then on to Baker Island Lighthouse. It was at Baker Island Lighthouse where his oldest son drowned. He then requested a transfer and was assigned back to Moose Peak Lighthouse. He was later transferred to Burnt Island Lighthouse in Boothbay Harbor where he served from 1936 until he retired in 1951. Photograph courtesy of Ann L. Muise.

This aerial image shows the large 1903 keeper's house that replaced the original keeper's house. Notice that the enclosed walkway to the tower is now gone, having been destroyed in a storm. It was replaced by a walkway with railings, which helped, but still made the hike to the lighthouse extremely difficult during storms with high winds and waves.

Coast Guardsman Danny Reid is shown here in boot camp at Cape May New Jersey in 1958. He later went on to serve as a Coast Guard keeper at Moose Peak Lighthouse, Whitlock's Mill Lighthouse, West Quoddy Head Lighthouse and at the Quoddy Head Life Boat Station in Lubec.

Coast Guard lighthouse keeper Danny Reid in the kitchen at Moose Peak Lighthouse in 1961. Acting as the station's cook, whatever he was making must have tasted mighty delicious out at the lighthouse. Photograph courtesy of Danny and Alice Reid.

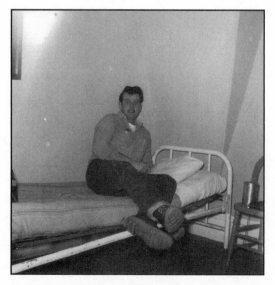

When lighthouse families no longer lived at Moose Peak Lighthouse, their personal home furnishings went with them. Coast Guard furnishings were much more institutional, as shown here, with Coast Guard keeper Danny Reid kicking back on the bunk at Moose Peak Lighthouse (circa 1961). This was a lot different than the lighthouse keepers had in earlier years. Photograph courtesy of Danny and Alice Reid.

Coast Guard lighthouse keeper Jimmy Olson and unknown keeper with dogs at Moose Peak Lighthouse (circa 1961). Photograph courtesy of Danny and Alice Reid.

It was not uncommon for families of Coast Guard keepers to visit Moose Peak Lighthouse. Lee Reid, mother of keeper Danny Reid, is on the 40 foot Coast Guard boat at Moose Peak Lighthouse (circa 1961). Photograph courtesy of Danny and Alice Reid.

Moose Peak Lighthouse Station as it appeared in 1961 when Danny Reid was stationed there. In 1982, the keeper's house, shown here, was blown up in a demolition exercise.

VIEW FROM MOOSE PEAK LIGHT, JONESPORT, ME.

Nice front view of the double keeper's house at Moose Peak Light Station from a vintage post card. These buildings no longer stand.

These solar panels now power the modern foghorn and the light in the tower at Moose Peak Lighthouse. The old fog signal building behind the solar panels is no longer used. The modern foghorn can be seen to the far right.

Today, Moose Peak lighthouse stands steadfast, and nearly forgotten in the pages of time, existing as a silent reminder of what was once a family lighthouse station on the rugged coast of Maine.

Narraguagus Lighthouse

Pond Island — Near Milbridge, Maine

Established in 1853 on the east side of Pond Island, near Milbridge, is the obscure Narraguagus Lighthouse. The lighthouse was built here to aid the many vessels than came and went here from the lumber industry.

Because it was built on Pond Island, it was often referred to as Pond Island Lighthouse, which can cause some confusion to the actual Pond Island Lighthouse that is located at the mouth of the Kennebec River near Popham Beach, Maine.

Originally the light station was built as a one family station, but in later years, an assistant keeper was added.

Stories and memories of the keepers and families that lived at Narraguagus Lighthouse are difficult to find. This could be because the lighthouse cannot be seen from the mainland and it was one of a number of Maine lighthouses that was discontinued in the 1930s. However, for 81 years a lighthouse keeper staffed the station. When it was discontinued it was sold and has remained privately owned ever since.

The original Narraguagus Lighthouse was built in 1853. The house was actually built around the tower. In 1875, the house was demolished, leaving the tower standing by itself and new buildings were constructed.

Narraguagus Lighthouse as it appeared with its second keeper's house. If you look closely you will notice a hand rung fog bell hanging from a metal holder and the lighthouse keeper is looking up at something in the tower. In this image the shades in the lantern room were closed to protect the Fresnel lens from the rays of the sun.

Look closely and you will notice a round outdoor cistern next to the tower that was used to collect rainwater from the roof. Obviously, this would only be effective in warm weather, as it would freeze in the winter months.

Narraguagus Lighthouse from the water as it appears today, having changed very little over the years. It is now privately owned.

Nash Island Lighthouse

Southeast Entrance to Pleasant Bay — South Addison, Maine

Nash Island Lighthouse was established in 1838 to mark the southeast entrance to Pleasant Bay off the coast of Addison, Maine. Although a number of keepers lived at the 16-acre station with their families, much of the island's history is yet to be rediscovered.

However, a good account of family life at the lighthouse was saved in the memories of Jenny Purington Cirone, whose father, John Purington, was the keeper of the lighthouse from 1916 to 1935. Many of these memories were documented in a film produced by Michel Chalufour called "Jenny's Island Life," which is available from the Friends of Nash Island Light, which is the group that now cares for the tower.

The light station was automated in 1947 and keepers were removed from the island. After automation, the Coast Guard destroyed the keeper's house and all other buildings, leaving only the tower.

Today the island is part of the Maine Coastal National Wildlife Refuge. Under the Maine Lights Program ownership of the lighthouse tower was awarded to the Friends of Nash Island Lighthouse.

Nash Island Lighthouse received its name because the land where the light station was built was purchased from the Nash family. As was typical of some of the early lighthouses, the first Nash Island Lighthouse was poorly constructed and numerous complaints were given, which were followed by numerous repairs. In 1856 the original lamps and reflectors were replaced by a Fresnel lens. However, the lighthouse continued to have problems and the structure, shown here, was torn down in 1874 and replaced by a square tower.

An unidentified lighthouse keeper is shown here by the station's boat and the very long boat ramp that was required to accommodate the tidal changes. The original boathouse was of the early typical design that was also used at other lighthouses.

In 1888, a pyramid fog bell tower was added to the responsibilities of the lighthouse keeper at Nash Island Lighthouse. In this image, the drapes are closed in the lantern room and a ladder is propped up against the tower indicating that the keeper was painting the structure.

The initials of H. A. Holt were inscribed on this rock at Nash Island with what appears to be the date of June 7, 1887. It may have been etched by an ancestor of Allen Carter Holt who served here as a lighthouse keeper some 23 years later. Photograph by Marilee Lovitt.

Lighthouse keeper Allen Carter Holt, his wife, and the lighthouse dog are shown here, keeping a watchful eye on their children. Holt, who served here from 1910 to 1916, with the help of his children, conducted a bird nesting count for the Audubon Society.

Antique post cards, such as this one of Nash Island Lighthouse, are often the best-recorded architectural history of some lighthouse stations.

John Purington is shown holding one of his nine children at Nash Island Lighthouse where he served as the keeper from 1916 to 1935. Previously, he was a lighthouse keeper at Deer Island Thorofare Lighthouse on Mark Island from 1912 to 1916, and at Whitehead Lighthouse, as an assistant keeper, from 1909 to 1911. He also served at Egg Rock Lighthouse. Photograph courtesy of Eva Denny.

Ellen Purington, wife of lighthouse keeper John Purington, raised nine children on island lighthouses during the time of the Great War (WWI), as well as during the Great Depression. Since her children had nothing but fond memories of island lighthouse life, she apparently managed her household duties, family life, and lighthouse responsibilities extremely well. Photograph courtesy of Eva Denny.

Genevieve "Jenny," Cirone, daughter of Nash Island lighthouse keeper John Purington, had very fond memories of living on Nash Island, where, by the age of ten, she had her own lobster traps. As a young girl she also started to raise sheep on the island, something she continued to do for her entire life. Later in life, she bought part of the island and the other nearby island to raise her sheep. One time a lady called her and wanted to purchase the island. She told Jenny, "Price was no object," to which Jenny replied, "Yes, you're right, price is no object, the island isn't for sale-at any price." Photograph courtesy of Eva Denny.

Spending 19 years on Nash Island, this was the only place that most of the Purington children ever knew as home. Four of the Purington boys, are shown here, showing off their shooting skills that they learned from their father, who was an avid hunter. One of the youngest boys, not yet allowed to shoot, can be barely seen sitting behind them.

In the winter months, when flocks of ducks or geese would appear, they would shoot as many of them as they could. They would clean and store them in the boathouse where they would remain frozen until they could be used for dinner.

Jenny recalled that she and her brothers rarely left the island to attend school; instead a traveling teacher would visit them on the island. However, Jenny later recalled that her older brothers would marry them as fast as a new one came, leaving a shortage of teachers. Photograph courtesy of Eva Denny.

Nash Island Lighthouse as it appeared during the tenure of John Purington, when he served there as the lighthouse keeper from 1916 to 1935. Photograph courtesy of Eva Denny.

Lighthouse keeper John Purington, on Nash Island, with his daughter Genevieve "Jenny." Photograph courtesy of Eva Denny.

Lighthouse keeper John Purington with some of his sons during the haying season. It was almost like living on a farm. All of the hay had to be cut and bundled by hand to be stored for the winter season. Photograph courtesy of Eva Denny.

With nine children on the island, it was never difficult to get a game of baseball started, something the family did quite often on Nash Island. Photograph courtesy of Eva Denny.

With nine hungry children to feed and the frequent guests that would visit Nash Island, the Purington family depended on hunting and a large number of lobster traps for food. They also sold lobsters to supplement their income. They followed a strict lobstering season as shown here by the lobster traps piled on the island. Jenny Purington Cirone (1912-2004), daughter of lighthouse keeper John Purington, said she started lobstering when she was ten years old, a trait she inherited from her father. In fact, she was out in her lobster boat pulling in traps in August of 2003, only a few short months before she died in February of 2004.

Members of the Purington family with the island cows and other animals on the island. Animals were the family's lifeline that they depended on for eggs, milk and meat.

Another view of Nash Island Lighthouse from the time John Purington was the keeper. Jenny Purington Cirone recounted in later years how it was the Purington children's responsibility to help paint all of the buildings, including the bell tower and the lighthouse tower. One particular year, Jenny painted the entire lighthouse tower by herself while her father hoisted her up the side of the tower in a bosun's chair.

Lighthouses of the Sunrise County

One day while Nash Island Lighthouse keeper, John Purington, was out tending his traps, he was informed that the lighthouse inspector was on his way. Purington rushed back to the island. As the inspector landed, Purington had no time to change and he had to put on his uniform, over his work clothes. The inspector gave him an excellent report; in fact it was the best report he had ever been given. Upon leaving the island, the inspector looked at him with a smile, and said, "Now you can take your uniform off from over those work clothes." It seems the inspector had known all along. Purington's wife decided they should take this picture to remind them of that special inspection day. Photograph courtesy of Eva Denny.

Lighthouse keeper John Purington is shown here kneeling with some of his children. Notice one of the family cows behind them by the lighthouse. The family depended on the cows for fresh milk for the family. Photograph courtesy of Eva Denny.

Earl Purington, youngest son of lighthouse keeper John Purington, joined the Coast in hopes that he would eventually be assigned to a lighthouse station. Photograph courtesy of Eva Denny.

Milking the cow on Nash Island was just one of the many family chores required of the children of lighthouse keeper John Purington.

Eleanor "Nellie" Copp and Edwin A. Pettegrow served at Nash Island Lighthouse in the 1930s. During Edwin's tenure as a lighthouse keeper, he also served at a number of other Maine lighthouses where his family was allowed to live with him. These included, Little River Lighthouse, Avery Rock Lighthouse, Petit Manan Lighthouse and Matinicus Rock Lighthouse, all in Maine, and, at the Isles of Shoals Lighthouse in New Hampshire. Some records have his last named incorrectly spelled as Pettigrew. Photograph courtesy of Eva Belanger.

At age 16, Farrell Pettegrow, son of lighthouse keeper Edwin A. Pettegrow, is shown here from the time he was stationed at Nash Island Lighthouse, wearing his father's lighthouse keeper's hat and jacket. Obviously, the photograph was not taken at the lighthouse. If the lighthouse inspector had seen Pettegrow's son wearing the lighthouse keeper's uniform, there would have been a serious repri-mand. Photograph courtesy of Farrell Pettegrow.

Nash Island Lighthouse from a photograph taken by lighthouse keeper Edwin Arthur Pettegrow during the 1930s when he was stationed there. He was proud of the fact that he, and his family, took good care of the government property.

During the tenure of keeper Edwin Pettegrow at Nash Island Lighthouses in the 1930s, the keeper's family rescued and nursed an injured owl back to health. Apparently the owl liked the care it had been given, because after it healed, the feathered creature decided to stay around as the lighthouse station's mascot. Photograph courtesy of Eva Belanger.

Larson Alley Sr. who served as the keeper at Nash Island in the 1940s. Like many other island keepers, he wanted fresh milk for his wife Edna and son, Larson Alley, Jr.

So, he took the lighthouse station's peapod (boat), and went to South Addison on the mainland, in search of a cow. Upon buying the cow, he returned to the boat landing with the cow. When a few of the local fisherman saw him with the cow, they inquired as to how he expected to get it to the island. As they all looked at the cow, one fisherman exclaimed, "Not in that peapod!" Another said that either the cow would fall out of the boat and drown, or it would capsize the boat, and they'd both drown."

Alley was not to be intimidated. He calmly took one look at the cow and said, "Okay Bessie, let's get in the boat," and he gently tugged at the cow, and the four legged animal, calmly stepped into the boat. As the fishermen watched in amazement, Alley, and the cow, now standing up in the peapod, made the trip to the island. Upon arriving on the island, Alley tried the same tactic, and said, "Okay, Bessie, get out of the boat, you're at your new home." As he gently pulled at the cow, even he was surprised, as the animal gracefully stepped out of the boat and onto the island. It seemed as if the cow really wanted to be there, at its new island home.

After serving at Nash Island Lighthouse Alley was transferred to Moose Peak Lighthouse.

Interestingly, many years later, Larson Alley's son, Larson Alley, Jr. joined the Coast Guard, and like his father before him, also served as a lighthouse keeper. As well as serving at the Fletcher Neck Life Boat Station in Biddeford Pool he served as a relief lighthouse keeper at Nubble Light in York, Goat Island Light in Kennebunkport, Wood Island Light in Biddeford Pool, Cuckolds Light in Boothbay Harbor and six months as Officer in Charge at Libby Island Lighthouse. Larson Alley, Jr.(r), is shown here in Saigon, South Vietnam will Bill Carter before he returned stateside, to lighthouse duty.

After Nash Island Lighthouse was automated and the keepers removed, the government abandoned the keeper's house. Instead of trying to find a new owner or caretaker for the beautiful keeper's house that had once had been the happy home for so many lighthouse keepers and families, the Coast Guard decided to burn the house and other buildings on the island.

As the fire consumed the house, the winds picked up and the fire began to spread across the island, burning the grazing land that Jenny Cirone needed for her sheep. She demanded that the Coast Guard stop the fire from spreading, informing them that she owned most of the island. But the officer in charge told her point blank it was not his problem, and in fact he didn't believe she owned any part of the island.

Jenny immediately went to the mainland and called the Coast Guard Admiral who immediately dispatched three Coast Guard boats, whose sailors, spent the next two days fighting the fire.

Jenny said at that time, she was more concerned about the grazing land being burned, which was needed for her sheep, than she was about the house being destroyed. However, in later years she firmly believed that the Coast Guard could have done something to save the house, rather than destroy the home that she and her family had lived in for so many years. Photograph courtesy of Eva Denny.

The gravestone of Leona Berry, daughter of Edna, and stepdaughter of Larson Alley, Sr., at the Bay View Cemetery overlooking Masons Bay in Jonesport, Maine. The love for Nash Island Lighthouse, where her stepfather and mother lived and she visited often, is obvious by the engraving on the stone.

This memorial on the island honors the memory of Clifford M. Purington, one of the children of lighthouse keeper John Purington. After Clifford's death, his sister, Jenny Cirone, would often come to meditate and remember her family's wonderful lighthouse life. After her death, Jenny's ashes were scattered near this site. Photograph courtesy of Eva Denny.

When the Coast Guard removed the light from the tower at Nash Island Lighthouse in 1982, they planned to tear the tower down. However, that plan must have been too expensive. Then they decided that it would be cheaper to blow up the tower and made an announcement, stating their intentions to the public. Believing that the lighthouse would soon be lost forever, Nick Salata, took this photo in 1982, so that the lighthouse could be remembered from its last year of standing. Fortunately, after receiving a large number of written and verbal protests, the Coast Guard changed its mind, and they let the tower stand.

In 1998, under the Maine Lights Program, ownership of Nash Island Lighthouse was transferred to the Friends of Nash Island, who have restored the tower, and now care for its long-term maintenance.

Volunteers from the Friends of Nash Island Lighthouse working on the restoration of the tower, in August of 1999. Photograph courtesy of Marilee Lovitt.

Jenny Cirone, daughter of lighthouse keeper John Purington, was widely respected and loved by the local community. She is shown here in a parade, on a float, with a replica of Nash Island Lighthouse. Also on the float, were some of her sheep, from the large herd that she was raising on the island. Although she loved all animals, the sheep were her favorite. Photograph courtesy of Eva Denny.

Jenny Cirone, is shown here in later years, tending to her lobster traps. As well as raising sheep, she spent nearly her entire life lobstering in the waters off Nash Island Lighthouse, where she had grown up. Photograph courtesy of Eva Denny.

Petit Manan Lighthouse

Milbridge, Maine

Under an Act of Congress dated April 27, 1816, the Petit Manan Lighthouse Station became the 8th lighthouse in Maine and 39th lighthouse in the United States. Construction was completed 1817 on the sixteen acre island near five intersecting bays close to the community of Milbridge. The first lighthouse tower was 25 feet tall and it was extensively rebuilt between 1823 and 1825.

The second tower, built between 1854 and 1855, was approximately 119 feet tall, and is the second tallest lighthouse in Maine and one of the four tallest in New England. It is a near twin to Boon Island Lighthouse off the coast of York and Kittery, Maine. However, very few people have ever seen it and fewer have ever visited the island. During its heyday, it was quite an important and active station, with three lighthouse keepers assigned to the station, all of who lived there with their families.

Although not all historians may agree, the first woman lighthouse keeper in U.S. history to be paid by the federal government served at Petit Manan Lighthouse. In the 1830s Robert Leighton was the keeper. For reasons unknown, Leighton abandoned his post in 1831 and left the lighthouse to be run by his wife, Jane, and son. He returned in 1832 but died shortly thereafter. Upon his death, Leighton's wife officially applied for the position of keeper, but Patrick Campbell received the appointment. However, during part of the time that Jane Leighton staffed the station, the federal government officially paid her, which would make her the first federally paid female lighthouse keeper in American history.

The light in the tower was originally lit by using whale oil, which was replaced by colza, then lard oil, and in 1917 by kerosene. In 1938 electricity came to the island and the light was powered by electric bulbs of 330,000-candle power, making it the second most powerful light on the Maine coast.

When Petit Manan Lighthouse was automated in 1972, it was still a three-man station, staffed by the Coast Guard, but wives and family members were not allowed to live on the island during that time. During automation, the gigantic 2nd order Fresnel lens was removed from the tower and is now on display at the Maine Lighthouse Museum in Rockland. A modern optic is now in the tower. Also for reasons unknown, when the station was automated, the cast iron gargoyles were removed. One of them is now on display at the Maine Lighthouse Museum, but what happened to the others is unknown.

The first fog bell was installed in 1855. In 1868 it was replaced by a 1,500-pound hand-rung fog-bell, which is now on display outside the elementary school in Milbridge. A steam fog signal was added in 1869, replaced in 1889 and rebuilt in 1892, and finally replaced in 1938 by a diaphragm air-horn.

Coal was used to fuel the fog signal boilers and to heat the homes. In 1889, in order to get the coal from the landing site to the buildings, a 760-foot of railroad-style tramway was built. This was replaced by a wooden walkway after electricity reached the station in the late 1930s.

The 16-acre island and the lighthouse are now part of the Maine Coastal Islands National Wildlife Refuge and are off limits to the public during the nesting season from April 1 to August 31 each year.

This is the only known photograph, believed to have been taken in 1870, that shows what was left of the first Petit Manan light tower. Built in 1817, the rubble-stone tower was 25 feet high and was lit by whale oil lamps in front of reflectors. The tower was apparently poorly constructed and it was totally renovated in 1823 and 1825. The tall tower shown here, which still stands today, was constructed in 1854-1855 and was built to replace the shorter tower.

Lighthouse keeper William D. Upton is shown here in his younger years. He served as an assistant keeper at Petit Manan from 1885 to 1890 and as Head Keeper from 1890 to 1901. Photograph courtesy of Gail Upton Denbow.

Unidentified ighthouse keeper who served at Petit Manan. Photograph courtesy of Gail Upton Denbow.

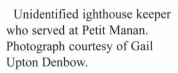

Petit Manan Lighthouse as it appeared in the time William D. Upton was keeper, circa 1900.

It is not known where this photograph was taken of lighthouse keepers (l-r) Lewis Sawyer, Adelbert Leighton and Heber Sawyer. Although Lewis Sawyer and his son Heber Sawyer were not stationed at any of the lighthouses mentioned in this book, they were stationed at a number of Maine lighthouses including Bear Island and Egg Rock Lighthouses. However, Adelbert Leighton was stationed at Petit Manan from 1891 to 1896.

Edmund Conners became a 2nd assistant keeper at Petit Manan in 1893. He was promoted to 1st assistant on August 15, 1896 and served through the end of the first quarter of 1903. Photograph courtesy of Carol Moffatt.

It is believed, but not confirmed, that George S. Conners (1860-1914), shown here, and who was the brother of Edmund Conners, was also stationed at Petit Manan Lighthouse. Some records show his last named spelled slightly differently as Connors. However, it is known that he was a 2nd assistant keeper at Whitehead Lighthouse from 1899 to 1902 and a keeper at Baker Island Lighthouse from 1902 to 1912. Photograph courtesy of Carol Moffatt.

Harry B. Collins was appointed 2nd assistant keeper at Petit Manan on November 6, 1897 apparently to replace Edwin Dustin Small who had requested a transfer. Photograph courtesy of Carol Moffatt.

Edward S. Farren served as a 2nd assistant keeper at Petit Manan from 1898 to 1901. Photograph courtesy of Ken Strout.

Before Frank L. Cotton was transferred to Petit Manan Lighthouse, he served at Spring Point Ledge Lighthouse in South Portland, Maine. As a young man, Cotton was considered one of the best baseball players in Maine. He also won medals as a gymnast, runner and as a member of the Dirigo Rowing Team and the Turnerein Bicycle Club. After Petit Manan, he went on to serve first as the assistant and then as the Head Keeper at Cape Elizabeth Two Lights from 1909 to 1912.

Under a new awards program adopted by the U.S. Lighthouse Service in 1912, he became the first lighthouse keeper to be awarded the Efficiency Star and the right to display the U.S. Lighthouse Service pennant. Many years later, that pennant was donated to a museum in Portland that later went out of business and the whereabouts of the flag remains a mystery to this day. Photograph courtesy of the Cape Elizabeth Historical Society.

This photograph of Petit Manan Lighthouse was taken by Charles A Kenney in 1903 when he was the lighthouse keeper. Finding photographs of lighthouses that were actually taken by the lighthouse keeper are rare.

By 1917 Petit Manan Lighthouse Station was considered by the government as the most elaborate complex ever assembled on an offshore light in the state of Maine. Structures included the tower, one double house, one single house, a brick fog-signal building, oil house, three fuel houses, two storage sheds, one work house, a barn, a boat house and a boat slip.

Tragedy struck Petit Manan Lighthouse on December 29, 1916 when lighthouse keeper Capt. Eugene Ingalls launched the station's power-boat with plans to go and meet his wife (Inez Robinson Ingalls) at Moose Peak Lighthouse. She had been visiting her parents Herbert and Mary Robinson who were the keepers there, and where Ingalls himself had previously been a lighthouse keeper. He had a small boat in tow for an emergency. Shortly after he left the station, a gale developed and as the assistant keeper watched from the island, the station's powerboat suddenly disappeared in a swell. Ingalls' five-year old daughter had also been watching from shore. However, in the gale, it was unclear at that time if he had changed direction to seek shelter or gone back to Petit Manan, and since there was no telephone line at the lighthouse, nothing could be learned. It wasn't until January 2 that both the people on the mainland and those on the island realized that Ingalls had not arrived on the mainland or gone back to the island.

His brother, Captain Herman Ingalls of the U.S. Lighthouse Service tender *Ziziana*, when hearing report, spent hours cruising the area looking for him or some clue as to what might have happened. The lighthouse tender Hibiscus also joined in the search.

Several days later, the sides of the boat were found washed up at Libby Island Lighthouse. Interestingly, the keepers had previously been complaining to the lighthouse inspector that they felt the boat was unsafe. The government had ordered only minor repairs to the boat and had declined to replace it.

Eugene C. Ingalls is shown here with his wife Inez (Robinson) Ingalls, with daughter Rita Francis sitting on her lap and daughter Alison, who was born on March 29, 1912 at West Quoddy Head Lighthouse in Lubec where Ingalls was the assistant keeper at the time. Shortly after Alison's birth, Ingalls was transferred to Moose Peak Lighthouse. From Moose Peak he was transferred to Petit Manan Lighthouse, where at age 34 he tragically lost his life at sea. Eugene C. Ingalls was also the brother of Frank Ingalls who at the time was the lighthouse keeper at St. Croix Lighthouse.
Photograph courtesy Jean C. Budrow.

Captain Herman Ingalls, shown here, as captain of the Lighthouse Tender *Ziziana*, searched the waters off Petit Manan Lighthouse looking for his brother, lighthouse keeper Eugene Ingalls, who had drowned when his boat sank on his way to the mainland from Petit Manan Lighthouse in 1917. Captain Ingalls later became Superintendent of the Second Lighthouse District. Photograph courtesy of Lois E. Sprague.

Inez Beatrice Robinson Ingalls was the wife of lighthouse keeper Eugene Ingalls. She was no stranger to lighthouses. She was the daughter of veteran lighthouse keeper Herman Robinson who served at Lubec Channel Lighthouse, West Quoddy Head Lighthouse, Moose Peak Lighthouse, Pemaquid Point Lighthouse and Monhegan Lighthouse. She lived with her lighthouse keeper husband at West Quoddy Lighthouse where she had also lived as a lighthouse keeper's daughter. She became a young widow with two small children when her husband lost his life at Petit Manan Lighthouse. Photograph courtesy of Jean C. Budrow.

Rita Francis Ingalls was only a small child when her father, lighthouse keeper Eugene Ingalls, lost his life in 1917 at age 34, at Petit Manan Lighthouse. In spite of the tragedy, she grew up to love lighthouses and spent much of her time with her grandfather, lighthouse keeper Herbert Robinson, who served at many Maine lighthouses such as Moose Peak, Pemaquid Point, Monhegan and others. Photograph courtesy of Jean C. Budrow.

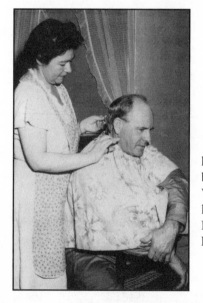

Lighthouse keepers could rarely make a trip to the barbershop for a haircut. On family stations, it was usually the lighthouse keeper's wife, between her many other chores, who also gave haircuts. Here, George Woodward's wife, Hazel, is using one of her adopted skills. Woodward later went on to serve as a lighthouse keeper at Franklin Island, Libby Island, Owls Head, and Wood Island, finishing his career at Rockland Breakwater in the mid 1940s.

George Woodward, a lighthouse keeper at Petit Manan in the 1920s is shown here lighting an oil lamp that was to be placed inside the Fresnel lens to illuminate the beacon. Although this particular photograph was taken of him at Owls Head Lighthouse, this same procedure was used when he was stationed at Petit Manan Lighthouse.

Lighthouse keeper James Freeman with his son Robert at Petit Manan in 1932. Freeman previously served as a lighthouse keeper at Plum Island Lighthouse in Newburyport, MA and at the Isles of Shoals Lighthouse, which is on an island off the coast of Portsmouth, NH. After living at Petit Manan Lighthouse for twelve years, Freeman received notice that he was to be transferred to Great Duck Island Lighthouse, also in Maine. The family left Petit Manan with heavy hearts. Freeman's daughter, Maizie, wrote in later years, "Tears were streaming down my face as I walked the path to the boat house for the last time." In 1939, while he was at Great Duck Island, the Lighthouse Service was dissolved and merged into the Coast Guard. Maizie Freeman, later in life wrote, "Soon after our arrival, the Coast Guard took over the running of the lighthouses and the old lighthouse keepers were gradually replaced by the Coast Guardsmen. My father was one of those replaced."

Children of lighthouse keeper James H. Freeman, Catherine and Maizie at Petit Manan Lighthouse in 1934. Catherine recalled in later years how she climbed the tower with her father as the sun was setting to light the lantern. While waiting for the last rays of the sun to disappear before lighting the lens, they stood on the outside platform. She said, "I would stand there with my Dad, and I remember wondering if the stillness of the view made him feel as I did – sad, as though we were the last people left on earth."

In 1947, Maizie Freemen, who was born on an island lighthouse, grew up on an island lighthouse with her lighthouse keeper family, married a Coast Guardsman who later became a lighthouse keeper at Boston Lighthouse, which is America's first light station. They lived at the lighthouse with their three children and a fourth was born while they were living there.

James Jr. and Robert, children of keeper James H. Freeman, from a 1930s image. One summer day President Franklin Roosevelt's boat came past the lighthouse and keeper Freeman took the children out to get a closer look, so they could wave at the president. Jim Jr. waved his cap so enthusiastically that he lost it overboard. They couldn't locate it. So, keeper Freeman explained that the hat was safe, that the president had plucked it out of the water and was wearing it. However, that didn't placate Jim Jr., he was mad at the president for many years, until he old enough to know better.

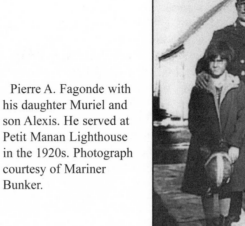

Pierre A. Fagonde with his daughter Muriel and son Alexis. He served at Petit Manan Lighthouse in the 1920s. Photograph courtesy of Mariner Bunker.

Augustus S. Kelly served at Petit Manan from 1925 to 1931.

In this image of Petit Manan Lighthouse, if you look closely, you can see a cow grazing on the grounds. In 1936, after four months of tedious work, a telephone line was brought to Petit Manan from Milbridge. On August 7th of that year the keepers and their families were able to communicate for the first time with the outside world.

Keepers and their families. Shown from left to right are: assistant keeper Augustus Kelly holding his son Albert, Bessie Kelley, Gracie Fagonde, head keeper Pierre Fagonde, Alma Bunker and assistant keeper Irv Bunker. Photograph courtesy of Mariner Bunker.

The keepers take a moment from work to pose for this photograph. (l-r) Keeper Augustus Kelley, head keeper Pierre Fagonde and assistant keeper Earl Ashby. Ashby later went on to serve at Lubec Channel Lighthouse from 1933 to 1939. Photograph courtesy Mariner Bunker.

Roscoe L. Fletcher was a lighthouse keeper at Petit Manan Lighthouse from 1928 to 1936. Roscoe and his wife Dorothy had two small children. They entertained themselves playing musical instruments and writing letters to family and friends on the mainland. Dorothy enjoyed playing the violin as well as the piano that was brought to the island. Dorothy recalled in later years that she would often get up at night with her husband to join him when it was his turn to do the night watch, smiling, as she said, "Just to torment him." The Fletchers left Petit Manan when Roscoe was promoted and transferred to become the head lighthouse keeper at Matinicus Rock Lighthouse where he was stationed at from 1936 to 1944. He retired shortly thereafter because of back injury.

Don and Trudy Ashby from a 2007 photograph by Ron Pesha. Don served as a Coast Guard keeper at Petit Manan Lighthouse, where is father before him served as a keeper in 1929 with the U.S. Lighthouse Service.

Beginning on September 15, 1953, Don Ashby served as keeper at West Quoddy Head Lighthouse and served there for three years. Interestingly, his father, Earle also served at West Quoddy Head Light as the assistant keeper from 1939 to 1942. After being transferred from West Quoddy Head Light, Don was stationed at Moose Peak Lighthouse and from there he was stationed at the nearby Cross Island Life Boat Station. He eventually went back to West Quoddy as Assistant Group Commander.

By the time this photograph was taken, the second keeper's house at Petit Manan had been demolished.

The spiral staircase inside the tower at Petit Manan Lighthouse in 1994. Photograph by Paula Roberts.

The iron tie rods on Petit Manan Lighthouse were installed in 1887 to strengthen the tower and keep it from swaying in high winds and storms. Today it stands as a monument to a lost era of maritime history.

St. Croix River Lighthouse

Dochet Island, Maine

Established in 1856, the St. Croix River Lighthouse gained its greatest notoriety from the written memories of Connie Small in her book, *The Lighthouse Keeper's Wife.*

The island's rich history, although quite famous, unfortunately seems to have been forgotten by most Americans. The island was originally named Muttoneguis by the Passamaquoddys. When the French first settled on the island in 1604, sixteen years before the Pilgrims landed at Plymouth, they named it St. Croix Island. It was here that the first Christmas celebration was held in America. However, the French explorers suffered a great loss of life due to scurvy and eventually abandoned the settlement.

In 1797 a boundary dispute was settled, officially making the six and a half acre island a part of the United States. Even in this part of North America, erosion has been a problem and the island is now much smaller than it originally was. In fact, after erosion exposed many of the graves on the island, it was often referred to as Bone Island. Over time it has also been called Demont's Island after Pierre Dugua de Monts, the man who was the leader of the first settlement. It later became known as Doucett Island which eventually evolved into the name that it has today: Dochet Island. However, to make matters more confusing, when the government sent out an announcement to mariners that the lighthouse had been established in 1856, W. B. Franklin, the lighthouse engineer who sent out the notice, said the lighthouse was built on Big Island.

The first keeper was Elias Barber who was took the position on Dec. 15, 1856. He served until the lighthouse was discontinued on August 1, 1859. A caretaker lived on the island, which was dark for ten years, until it was reestablished in October of 1869. Subsequent U.S. Lighthouse Service keepers were Jacob F. Young from November 1869 to December, 1874; Harrison Keen from January 1875 to April 1880; Joseph Huckins from May 1880 to February 1903, Walden B. Hodgkins from April 1903 to October 1905; Frank Jellison from October 1905 to May 1912, Frank Ingalls from May 1912 to October 1923, and Charles A. Kenney from 1923 to 1930. He was followed by Elson Small from 1930 to 1939 when the Lighthouse Service was dissolved and merged into the Coast Guard. All of the keepers after 1939 were Coast Guard personnel. Elson Small joined the Coast Guard and, with the exception of a brief interruption during those Coast Guard years, he continued to serve at St. Croix until 1946 when he was transferred. Coast Guard keeper Everett Quinn replaced Small and served until 1954 when the St. Croix Lighthouse was automated.

Captain Charles A. Kenney, who had served with distinction at other Maine lighthouses, came to St. Croix River Lighthouse in October of 1923 and served here until his retirement at age 70 in 1930. Kenney's sister, Anges "Aggie" Cole, spent six months on the island lighthouse from October 1929 to June of 1930. During that time she wrote a daily journal of life at the lighthouse, which, as indicated from her writings, was very satisfying to those who lived there. Unlike some remote and dangerous lighthouses along the Maine coast, the keepers here enjoyed a pretty normal life and spent many of their evenings playing various card games. They were also great letter writers and one of the highlights of life was the arrival of the mail. The worst time of the year was the winter months when they were literally trapped in the house for days on end and all they would hear is the howling of the wind and everything around them was pure white with snow.

In 1949 the island was designated the Saint Croix Island National Monument. Years later, in October of 1966, it was listed on the National Register of Historic Places. However, after the station was automated in 1957, it was left abandoned to the elements. Plans to turn the lighthouse into a museum never materialized. In 1976 some young people, while camping on the island, are believed to have started a fire in the stove, but the chimney was blocked up. The fire soon got out of control and the historic structure, which was listed as the First Lighthouse in the First Coast Guard District of the United States of America, was destroyed and lost forever.

In 1984 Congress took an additional step to protect the island when they designated it an International Historic Site, which is a unique designation in the National Park Service. However, it was far too late for the lighthouse, which had been destroyed eight years earlier.

The first St. Croix River Lighthouse, built in 1856, lasted until 1901.

This photograph taken in 1885 shows the complete St. Croix River Light Station. Quite evident are the boathouse, barn and a very crude tripod that was used for the fog bell.

In 1901 the St. Croix River Light Station was entirely rebuilt. The second structure was very similar to the first house, but did have its differences. Over time, some additions were added to the house.

Side view of the St. Croix River Lighthouse. Notice the back room addition and the nice bay windows. The year of this photograph is unknown.

Frank N. Jellison, shown here, had an illustrious career in the United States Lighthouse Service and was the keeper at St. Croix Lighthouse from 1905 to 1909. He had previously been an assistant keeper at Whitehead Lighthouse from 1890 to 1892 and then Head Keeper at Whitehead form 1892 to 1905. After St. Croix, he became the keeper at Whitlock's Mill Lighthouse from 1909 to 1920. The letter K on his uniform indicated that he was a Head Keeper.

Charles A. Kenney was the keeper at the St. Croix Lighthouse from 1923 to 1930 when this photo was taken by a relative who wrote on the back of the photos, "This is Dochet Lighthouse, a place of pleasant memories."

Lighthouse keeper Elson Small was no fan of canned milk, preferring instead the taste of fresh milk from a cow. So he built a barge of sorts, went to the mainland and bought a cow, which he transported back to the island on his barge. One day in 1945 when the lighthouse inspector arrived on the island, he saw Elson milking, Blossom the cow, and got very excited. He immediately sent one of the men back to the lighthouse tender to get his camera and took a number of photographs. Since the Lighthouse Service was always looking for good men to become keepers, he thought the photograph would make a good recruitment poster. Although the poster was never made, the image was widely circulated to the media and appeared in newspapers across the country, gaining more attention for the Lighthouse Service than the inspector ever imagined.

Shortly after arriving at St. Croix River Lighthouse on Dochet Island in 1930, Elson and Connie Small decided to plant a large garden. Elson decided he needed a plow of some sorts, as well as some easier form of transportation to get around the island. He eventually found an old Model T on the mainland. Although there wasn't much left of it, he got it to the island and got it working again. This was the first of several old vehicles he brought to the island and rebuilt. Elson is shown here in the driver's seat transporting the old jalopy to the island. A friend of his is shown leaning against the vehicle.

Remembering that there were no roads on the island, Elson's sense of humor is shown here with one of the old vehicles that he brought to the island.

The only power that Elson Small had on the island when he was the lighthouse keeper came from batteries that had to be brought from the mainland. So Elson and his brother-in-law built a windmill to generate power. This was surely the first lighthouse in America to generate power from the wind.

Connie and Elson Small pose with Connie's brother, Gerald Scovill and his wife Grace, at the memorial plaque that was placed on the island in 1904 honoring the 300th anniversary of the discovery and occupation of the island, which was the only settlement of Europeans at the time north of Florida.

In 1939 the United States Lighthouse Service was dissolved and merged into the Coast Guard. Lighthouse keepers were given the option of joining the Coast Guard or staying on as civilian keepers. Although the keepers throughout the country were evenly divided, Elson decided to join the Coast Guard. When his new uniform arrived, he took a moment to pose with his wife Connie for this photograph.

Connie Small and her husband enjoyed the "Lum'n Abner" radio program that began airing in 1932 and stayed on the radio until 1954. In its early years, it was the highest rated program on radio. Connie wrote a letter to Chester Lauck and Norris Goff, who portrayed Columbus "Lum" Edwards and Abner Peabody on the program telling them how much she enjoyed the show from her tiny island on the Canadian and United States border where she lived as a lighthouse keeper's wife. Sometime later, much to her delight, she received a letter from them with an autographed photograph.

It was December 9, 1941, just two days after America had been attacked at Pearl Harbor, when businessmen from Calais came to Dochet Island and asked lighthouse keeper Elson Small if they could chop down a tree and send it to the White House for Christmas. It was thought that by sending a Christmas tree from the island where the first Christmas in America was celebrated in 1604 would be a great tribute to America's morale and would be especially fitting at the time, since President Roosevelt was hosting Prime Minister Churchill at the White House.

St. Croix Lighthouse keeper Elson Small is shown here with his wife Connie holding the ax that was used to cut down the tree.

Elson and Connie Small in the winter of 1941 at St. Croix Lighthouse.

Some winters were worse than others at St. Croix River Lighthouse. Here Connie Small is shown in 1931 standing in front of icebergs that had built up along the shore.

Lighthouse keeper Elson Small is shown here at St. Croix Lighthouse with his good friends Dr. Willard Bunker and Robert Moore Brinkerhoff who was a noted syndicated cartoonist who, in 1917, created "Little Mary Mix-Up," which appeared in 100 newspapers until it ended with his retirement in 1956. During one visit by the men and their wives, knowing that blueberry pie was Brinkerhoff's favorite, Connie Small baked one especially for him. When Connie went to get the pie off the windowsill where she had left it to cool she found that the cow Blossom, had her nose buried deep into the pie as it was being devoured. Looking at the cow with its face all blue, Brinkerhoff immediately started to sketch the cow, saying that as much as would have loved the pie, the scene was better, one that he could use in his comic strip. Perhaps this is what they were so jovial about when this photo was taken.

While stationed on St. Croix River Lighthouse, Elson Small made several boats. This was one of them that he built by hand.

Scottie the cat was a favorite pet of Elson and Connie Small while at St. Croix River Lighthouse. Connie had many fond memories of Scottie. At one point during World War II, they were told to close the light station and leave the island. Their temporary housing on the mainland was not appropriate for the cat, so Scottie went to live out the rest of his years on a farm.

Lighthouses of the Sunrise County

Lighthouse keeper Elson Small is shown here with a group of visitors to the lighthouse.

This view is from the later years of Elson and Connie Small's time at the lighthouse. Notice the adorable awnings on the house and the quaint white fence.

Unlike some of his friends who had decided to remain on a civilian lighthouse keepers when the Coast Guard took over the Lighthouse Service, Elson was proud of the fact that he decided to join the Coast Guard, and proud to wear its uniform, a decision he later regretted. He had assumed like all other dedicated and hardworking lighthouse keepers, that his job as a lighthouse keeper after so many years of faithful service was secure. Suddenly, without warning, on June 4, 1943, Bosun's Mate First Class Charles Whitney showed up at the lighthouse with orders that he was to relieve Elson who was being transferred to Eastport, Maine to take command of a patrol boat. They had three hours to leave St. Croix River Lighthouse and no arrangements were made for them to pack and move their belongings. This was something they were never told to expect when Elson transferred from a civilian keeper to a military keeper.

Connie was extremely upset, but Elson knew he had to follow orders. Eventually, they were able to move all their furniture and belongings off the island and into storage, then Elson was told he was again being transferred and was being shipped to New York. Fortunately, by chance, a superior officer found out how Elson had been treated and changed his orders and told him to report back to St. Croix Lighthouse and Bosun's Mate First Class Whitney was being transferred to the nearby Little River Lighthouse in Cutler.

They remained at St. Croix for another two years until Elson was again transferred, this time to the Portsmouth Harbor Lighthouse in New Hampshire where he would remain until his retirement from the Coast Guard. Connie recalled in later years that the best years of her life were at St. Croix River Lighthouse.

Launching or landing the boat at St. Croix was never easy, even in good weather as is shown here. However, it was the bad weather that caused problems. There were those perilous times when the boat capsized, nearly killing the keeper and causing the loss of valuable supplies. Here Elson Small is securing the boat on the boat ramp. He then used the winch to pull the boat, loaded with supplies, up into the boathouse. One of the original peapod boats used at St. Croix Lighthouse is now on display at the Penobscot Marine Museum in Searsport, Maine.

Louis S. and Constance Zawislak, shown here in their wedding photo taken in Eastport, Maine on Sept. 23, 1943, served as Coast Guard keepers on St. Croix Island Lighthouse during part of the time during World War II when Elson Small was assigned elsewhere, only to return later. Photograph courtesy of Louis T. Zawislak.

This aerial image of the St. Croix Light River Station was taken in 1950 as an official Coast Guard record of the station that they were planning to eventually automate. It shows a well-kept station and clearly shows the old pyramid structure that house the station's fog bell.

Veteran U.S. Lighthouse Service keeper Everett W. Quinn, who served from 1949 to 1954, was the last one to serve as a keeper at St. Croix River Lighthouse. He had previously served at Cuckolds Lighthouse, Mt. Desert Rock Lighthouse, and Manana Island Fog Signal Station. He is shown here in 1935 at Mt. Desert Lighthouse with fellow lighthouse keepers George York in the middle and Henly Day on the right. Photograph courtesy of Shirley Robinson.

Bill Townsend, while working for the National Park Service, took this photograph of St. Croix Lighthouse on a visit to the island in 1971. By that time the lens had been removed from the tower and the windows and shielding around the lantern room had numerous bullet holes. It wasn't long after this that the lighthouse was destroyed.

Connie Small is shown here in 2004 with the quilt she made depicting her life at St. Croix Lighthouse from 1930 to 1946. Upon her death, at the age of 103, the quilt was donated by her family to the American Lighthouse Foundation and is now in the collection of the lighthouse museum in Rockland, Maine.

West Quoddy Head Light

Lubec, Maine

The picturesque West Quoddy Head Lighthouse, located in Lubec, is the easternmost lighthouse on the mainland of the United States of America. Although it is one of the most recognizable lighthouses in New England, and perhaps America, because of its location, it is not the most visited.

West Quoddy Head Lighthouse Station was first established in 1808 on the eastern end of the head of land marking the west side entrance to what is called Quoddy Roads, overlooking the Bay of Fundy. It was built to warn vessels of the dangerous offshore ledge of rocks.

Like many early light stations in the United States, the first station at West Quoddy was poorly constructed. It was replaced in 1831 with a new tower. Early keepers complained about the poor construction of both the tower and the house. In the winter months, the inside of the tower was covered with ice from condensation, the windows leaked and the house was cold and damp and the chimneys had a downdraft that blew smoke back into the keeper's house. Fortunately, over the years numerous repairs were made, and in 1858 the tower was rebuilt.

As time progressed all of the recorded memories of all of the keepers and families that lived at West Quoddy always related to how wonderful life was at the lighthouse. And, indeed they did have it better than many lighthouse keepers who lived at some of Maine's remote offshore lighthouses. An example of this occurred in 1899, when West Quoddy Lighthouse keeper John W. Guptill was ordered transferred from West Quoddy to Avery Rock Lighthouse where he had previously been stationed. He refused to go.

In his letter of resignation he wrote, "After being in the service more than seventeen years and seven of them at Avery Rock, I can not go there again."

When it was announced that West Quoddy Lighthouse, as with all other lighthouses, would be automated and its keepers removed, the local community protested. But automation did arrive and lighthouse keepers would never again live at West Quoddy Head Lighthouse.

Under the Maine Lights Program ownership of the light station was transferred to the State of Maine and it is now part of Quoddy Head State Park.

In 1998 the West Quoddy Head Lighthouse Keepers Association was formed and today a dedicated group of volunteers operate a visitors center and museum in the restored keeper's house. In season, a park ranger lives on the second floor of the keeper's house.

Visitors to West Quoddy Head Lighthouse also have another treat. They are invited to walk the trails along the most spectacular cliff view on the Atlantic seaboard, more so than at any other lighthouse. Also there are trails that go through the bogs where plants survive on moisture rather than roots.

Just as West Quoddy Lighthouse Station was a wonderful family station for the keepers of yesteryear, it again beckons families to come to enjoy its unique part of history, beautiful scenery, and wonderful trails at the easternmost lighthouse on the mainland of the United States of America. It is here that the rays of the sun are the first to touch the mainland each and every day, even in the fog.

Shown here is the 1858 West Quoddy Head Lighthouse Station as it appeared in 1860. Although red stripes were painted on the tower shortly after it was built, it looks in pretty bad shape when this photograph was taken. The large tower to the left of the light-house was an early fog bell tower. Because of the heavy fog associated with the area, a number of different fog bells were tested here until a steam powered fog signal was installed in 1887.

This image of West Quoddy Lighthouse shows a walkway from the tower to what was probably one of the fog bell towers.

This early image from the water shows West Quoddy Head Light with a number of outbuildings and perhaps an early steam whistle house.

Shown here is Allison Jean Ingalls, who was born March 28, 1912 at West Quoddy Head Lighthouse when her father Eugene Ingalls was the assistant keeper there. Her father later transferred to Moose Peak Lighthouse and from there he was transferred to Petit Manan Lighthouse where his family lived with him on the island. In 1917, while Allison was on the mainland with her mother and sister, she watched her father's boat approaching when it suddenly disappeared. Her father's body was found a few days later and Allison and her family were forced to leave the lighthouse life that they loved so much. Photograph courtesy of Jean C. Budrow.

Mary Estelle Myers Robinson (1863-1952) wife of West Quoddy Lighthouse keeper Herbert Robinson, who served as a lighthouse keeper at West Quoddy from 1905 to 1907. Mary and Herbert Robinson's daughter, Inez, grew up to marry lighthouse keeper Eugene Ingalls, who also became a lighthouse keeper at West Quoddy, gave birth to Allison Ingalls at West Quoddy Head Light. Photograph courtesy of Jean C. Budrow.

This view from the water shows the new brick fog signal building.

Shown here are the crew from the West Quoddy Life Saving Station that was located near West Quoddy Head Lighthouse. Although the year of the photograph is unknown, it is obvious that it is an early image. The United States Life Saving Service was considered the sister organization of the United States Lighthouse Service. In 1915 the Life Saving Service and the Revenue Cutter Service were merged to create the United States Coast Guard. The lady holding the rolling pin could have been the wife of the head keeper of the station, or perhaps the station's cook. The original West Quoddy Life Saving Station was later replaced by other buildings that still stand today and is now operated as a bed and breakfast.

There was a large gathering of some kind in this 1909 image of the West Quoddy Life Saving Station located near West Quoddy Head Lighthouse. Clearly shown in the photograph is a large band from Lubec, a horse drawn carriage, some of the crew of the Life Saving Station, and a lighthouse keeper, perhaps from West Quoddy Head Light. The keepers of the Life Saving Station and the keepers of the lighthouse often worked closely together and became steadfast friends. Photograph courtesy of Judi Kearney.

Ephraim Johnson is shown here with his wife Ada on their 10th wedding anniversary. Ephraim arrived at West Quoddy in 1901 as the assistant keeper under principle keeper Warren Murch. In 1905 he was elevated to principle keeper, a position he held until 1931 when he retired at age 68. While at the lighthouse, Johnson and his family became very self sufficient and raised all of their own vegetables and enjoyed picking wild blueberries, raspberries and even cranberries.

In an article in *Lighthouse Digest* his granddaughter Gwen Wasson recalled that her grandfather always wore his light keeper's hat, even when he wore work clothes. She also recalled that he was a very religious man and the family traveled to church by horse and buggy and in the wintertime by sleigh. On Sunday afternoons the family gathered in the parlor at the lighthouse and played the pump organ and sang songs. Sometimes Johnson would also play the violin, which he was very good at. Johnson had a special knack for predicting snowstorms, something the locals always depended on. Every year he predicted how many snow storms the winter months would bring and for many years he never missed the number by more than one.

Eugene Larrabee, a veteran lighthouse keeper who had previously served at Franklin Island Lighthouse, became the principle keeper at West Quoddy Head Lighthouse Head Lighthouse when Ephriam Johnson retired in 1931. He is shown here with an unidentified person, who might be an employee of the United States Lighthouse Service.

West Quoddy lighthouse keeper Eugene Larrabee with his granddaughter Sandra, who was raised at West Quoddy Head Lighthouse. Larrabee made the cart that Sandra is riding in. Notice the clothesline with the clothes blowing in the wind. The lighthouse was a well-maintained family station in those days.

Shown is here is Frank Larrabee, son of lighthouse keeper Eugene Larrabee at West Quoddy Head Lighthouse with his wife Alda. Frank grew up at Petit Manan Lighthouse where his father had previously been a lighthouse keeper. Alda Larrabee died twelve days after giving birth to Sandra Larrabee, who then spent her early years growing up at West Quoddy Head Lighthouse. Frank Larrabee stayed close at hand, holding jobs at the American Can Company and later at the *Lubec Herald* newspaper. In the days of the "New Deal" he found work installing metal fences with the Civilian Conservation Corps at Quoddy Head.

Eugene and Ethel Larrabee are shown here after retiring from West Quoddy Head Lighthouse. With them in the middle is Gilbert Larrabee. Lighthouse keeper Larrabee died in May of 1957.

Sandra Larrabee in 1939 at West Quoddy Head Lighthouse with one of the many wooden figurines that her grandfather, lighthouse keeper Larrabee made while stationed at West Quoddy Head Light. In later years she recounted, that in addition to his light keeping duties, her grandfather and her father maintained lobster traps. Her grandfather also raised chickens, and cared for the kitchen garden and his flowers, which he loved very much.

West Quoddy Head Lighthouse was popular back in 1948 as is evident from this cover of *Woman's Day* magazine.

Lighthouse keeper Howard, "Bob" Gray working on the equipment in the fog signal building at West Quoddy Lighthouse in the early 1950s. The compressor filled the white tank with compressed air that ran the foghorn that could be heard for 15 miles. Photograph courtesy of Pam Grindle and Dorothy Meyer.

This September 1945 cover of the *Saturday Evening Post* featured West Quoddy Head Lighthouse. Although this was an artist rendition, it clearly depicted lighthouse keeper Howard "Bob" Gray while doing lawn maintenance at the lighthouse. It also depicts the idyllic romantic lighthouse life of the type that many people dream about. Gray was the last keeper of the United States Lighthouse Service to be a keeper at West Quoddy Head Lighthouse. When the Lighthouse Service merged with the Coast Guard in 1939, lighthouse keepers were given the option of staying on as civilian keepers or joining the Coast Guard. Gray opted to join the Coast Guard. When he retired in 1952, it was the end of the era of the true lighthouse family living at West Quoddy Head Lighthouse.

West Quoddy Lighthouse in 1945. The barn at the far left, the work building in the middle and the small shed on the right, no longer stand. Look closely and you will see the old automobiles.

Earle Ashby, a veteran Maine lighthouse keeper, is shown here in his retirement years. As well as serving at a number of other Maine lighthouses, including Petit Manan and Lubec Channel Light from 1933 to 1939, he served at West Quoddy from 1939 to 1942. Later, his son, Don, also served as a keeper at West Quoddy Head Lighthouse. Photograph courtesy of Don Ashby.

This old post card image shows a tall chimney coming from the steam powered fog signal building at West Quoddy Head Light.

This 1940s image shows Coast Guardsman Nick Dowger at the fog signal building at West Quoddy Head Light. Notice the large foghorn protruding from the building.

One of the old compressors in the fog signal building as it appeared in the 1960s. Photograph courtesy of Ron Pesha.

This unusual view of West Quoddy Lighthouse showing a vintage automobile was taken in the 1950s. Photograph courtesy of Ron Pesha.

Bobby Gray, son of lighthouse keeper Howard Gray, poses for this photograph in the 1950's, probably to show off the new car. Howard Gray was keeper from 1934 to 1952.

This vintage, but modern era, photograph shows one of the station's fog bells on display on the lawn next to the white fence. Look closely in the tower and notice that the valuable Fresnel lens in the lantern room is covered. In earlier years drapes were used on the windows of the lantern room to protect the lens from the harmful rays of the sun.

Thomas L. Keene was a Coast Guard keeper at West Quoddy Head Light in the 1960s. He was also stationed at Whitlock's Mill and Little River lighthouses. Keene was a prolific writer and wrote a number of poems about the places where he was stationed. Photograph courtesy of Julie Keene.

Although the beam from West Quoddy Light, as well as the fog signal, warned mariners away from the dangerous ledges by the lighthouse, dangerous weather conditions still caused shipwrecks as shown here with the wreck of the *Lanie Cobb* at West Quoddy Head Lighthouse on September 10, 1915. Photograph courtesy of Julie Keene.

The Coast Guard crew at West Quoddy Head Lighthouse in the late 1970s. Unlike the days of old, West Quoddy Head Light, by this time, was not a family station. Shown left to right: BM1 Clifton Scofield, BM1 George "Bubba" Eaton, MK2 Carl Hatch and MK2 Dave Blanding. Photograph courtesy of George Eaton.

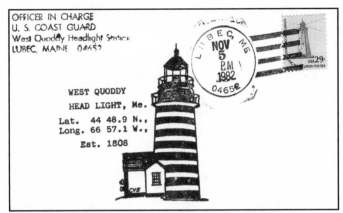

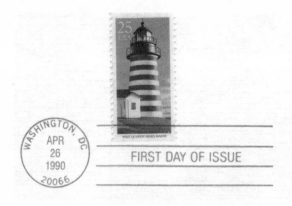

This rare envelope from the Officer In Charge at West Quoddy Head Lighthouse featuring the 29-cent Sandy Hook Lighthouse in New Jersey was postmarked in 1982.

In 1990 West Quoddy Head Lighthouse was featured on a United States postage stamp. However, the stamp featured the lighthouse with 12 stripes instead of its actual 15 stripes.

Aerial view of West Quoddy Head Lighthouse taken by the Coast Guard in 1951.

Lighthouse maintenance at a location like West Quoddy is on ongoing effort, as is shown in this 1985 photograph from *Maine's Working Coast* magazine.

The prep work for repainting the tower in 2003 first required an under-coating sealer that was a bluish gray color giving the lighthouse a much different appearance. Here the bottom three red stripes have already been painted, while the top stripes are still a bluish-gray making for an unusual photograph.

Standing exposed to the ocean and the harsh elements, old lighthouse towers require constant care. Here a workman is preparing the tower for painting in 2003.

Lighthouse keeper Howard "Bob" Gray is shown here at the automation ceremony at West Quoddy Head Light on June 30, 1988. He is wearing his old Coast Guard lighthouse keeper's hat. His father, Joseph Gray, had also been a lighthouse keeper and Bob followed in his footsteps and joined the U.S. Lighthouse Service in 1932. He served as an assistant lighthouse keeper at Boon Island Lighthouse. He was transferred to West Quoddy Lighthouse in April of 1934 and served there until his retirement in 1952 because of a health problem caused from an earlier fall at the lighthouse.

He and his wife Sarah, known as "Sadie," raised three children at West Quoddy, where his children later recalled that life was perfect for them and they wouldn't have traded those days for anything. He was the last keeper of the United States Lighthouse Service at West Quoddy Head Light. During the 1988 ceremony removing the last keepers, who were then Coast Guard keepers, forever from West Quoddy Head Light, Capt. John E. Williams, USCG, presented Gray with the last U.S. flag flown by the Coast Guard at West Quoddy Head Lighthouse. Gray passed away on July 5, 1994. Photograph courtesy of Pam Grindle and Dorothy Meyer.

In 1997 junior high school students from around the state, in a movement started and led by students from Noble Junior High School in the southern part of the state, campaigned for West Quoddy Lighthouse to be on the state's regular plate of issue. Although the students had the editorial support of all the TV stations and most of the newspapers in Maine, and they had a unanimous vote of approval in Maine's House of Representatives, the bill to issue the plate was voted down in Maine's State Senate in favor of a license plate featuring a chickadee.

Diana Wilson is holding a portrait of West Quoddy Head Light keeper Ephriam Johnson and his wife Ada from a painting done by Jane Dore in 2004 from a photograph from the collection of Gwen Wasson. The portrait is now hanging in the visitors center at West Quoddy Head Light.

West Quoddy Head State Park Ranger David Jones, with Connie Small, Maine's "First Lady of Light," and author of the book, *The Lighthouse Keeper's Wife*, at the lighthouse. In 1983 David Jones became the first non-lighthouse keeper to live in the keeper's house after the Coast Guard automated the lighthouse. This was of great historical significance since his great grandfather, Ephraim Johnson, was the lighthouse keeper here from 1901 to 1931 and David's cousin and an uncle tended the lighthouse in later years. Jones carried on his family's tradition at the lighthouse and cared for it as if it was his own. He delighted in talking with the tourists who visited the site. He was active in the efforts to create a visitors center at the lighthouse but he passed away suddenly at the age of 48 in 2001, before seeing the visitors center become a reality.

Gwen Wasson and Malcolm "Mac" Rouse at the June 19, 2004 West Quoddy Lighthouse annual celebration. Gwen's great grandfather was Ephraim Johnson, West Quoddy's light-house keeper from 1901 to 1931. Rouse was the last Coast Guard keeper, leaving in 1988 when the lighthouse was automated. Interestingly, Rouse was also the last Coast Guard keeper at Maine's Owls Head Lighthouse, near Rockland, Maine, leaving there when it was automat-ed in 1989. Photograph by Jeremy D'Entremont for *Lighthouse Digest.*

Lantern room restoration at West Quoddy Head Light in October of 2004. At this time the lantern room was in very poor condition and the copper dome had to be replaced. Other work done included replacing missing drain-spouts, repairing corroded cast iron framework, replacing all the lantern room glass and removal of lead paint and repairing the rusted areas of the deck. The $176,000 project was done by Campbell Construction Company.

On July 30, 2005, a granite marker was dedicated at West Quoddy Head Light, designating the spot as the Easternmost Point in the United States of America. At the time of the dedication, a time capsule was buried in front of the marker; it will be unearthed in 2058. Among those participating and speaking at the event was Tim Harrison, second from the right.

The late Ken Black, known as "Mr. Lighthouse," and the author (r) at West Quoddy Head Lighthouse in July of 2006.

Ken Black, "Mr. Lighthouse," with George "Bubba" Eaton at the West Quoddy Head Lighthouse annual celebration in 2006. Eaton was a Coast Guard keeper at the lighthouse from 1978 to 1982.

Chief Chuck Petronis, USCG, Aids To Navigation Southwest Harbor, with a piece of the original cupola of West Quoddy Head Lighthouse with a painting of the lighthouse done by Ron Frontin. The Coast Guard presented this work of art to CWO Kenneth Black, USCG, Ret., at a special dinner honoring Black on June 17, 2006. Black, known as, "Mr. Lighthouse," considered West Quoddy Head Light as his favorite beacon.

In July of 2007, during the 5th annual celebration of the opening of the Visitors Center at West Quoddy Head Light, a special cachet envelope and postmark honoring the late Kenneth Black, known by many as "Mr. Lighthouse," was issued. At one time Ken Black was Commander of Group Quoddy Head and West Quoddy Head Light was his favorite lighthouse. He founded the lighthouse museum in Rockland, Maine.

The gravestone of Russell W. Reilly features West Quoddy Head Lighthouse, where he served as a Coast Guard lighthouse keeper. Reilly also served at a number of other lighthouses, including Little River Lighthouse in Cutler, Libby Island Lighthouse in Machias Bay and Whitlock's Mill Lighthouse in Calais. Photograph by Kelly Reilly.

West Quoddy Head Light is as popular with tourists as it is with lighthouse aficionados. Here, members of the New England Lighthouse Lovers, a chapter of the American Lighthouse Foundation, posed with their banner at West Quoddy Head Lighthouse in July 2006.

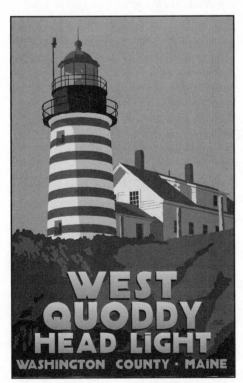

Retro poster design by Maine artist Alan Claude. www.AlanClaude.com

Proving the universal appeal of West Quoddy Head Lighthouse, this unique facsimile of West Quoddy Head Light is at Captain's Cove Seaport in Bridgeport, CT.

Quoddy Light

The great gray sea and the headland bold,
The tall gaunt tower of the lighthouse old,
The rhythmic beat of the waves below,
Gleaming white as the wintry snow.

The sunset flames and smoulders away,
Firing the sails in the lower bay;
And the beacon swings its burning light,
To misty sea and coming night.

And answering lights are kindled afar,
From rocky shore and from sandy bar,
That flush responsive and greetings send.
Burn on, Burn on, O signal light!

Fling out thy message to the night!
In darkness dense and danger's hour,
Thou art a mighty saving power.

Like loyal hearts that love and cling
Through all the ills that life can bring,
That shines forth with a beauty rare,
Through storms and shipwreck and despair.

This poem was pasted in a page of an old scrapbook with an image of West Quoddy Head Lighthouse and a caption that read, "Capt. Warren Murch of Quoddy Head Lighthouse with his wife and daughter are visiting friends in Jonesport and Ellsworth. Warren Murch was the keeper at West Quoddy Head Lighthouse from 1899 to 1905. There was no author given and only a statement that the poem was written, "For the Herald."

Whitlock's Mill Lighthouse

The Northernmost Lighthouse in New England — Calais, Maine

Although Whitlock's Mill Lighthouse is the northernmost lighthouse in New England, it is one of Maine's least known or written about lighthouses. This could be because it was located off the beaten lighthouse path, or perhaps because of the idyllic location where life was pretty normal for the lighthouse keepers.

The first use of a light here dates back to the late 1800s when the government owned a small piece of land where a lantern with a red lens was hung from a tree to mark the location on the south bank of the St. Croix River in the town of Calais which was a port of entry at the border with St. Stephen, New Brunswick, Canada. The first person assigned to keep the beacon lighted at night was Colfin Campbell Whitlock, a successful businessman who owned a lumbering operation and sawmill. The area eventually became known as Whitlock's Mill. Whitlock also owned the largest grocery store on the river and in his retirement years he operated a bookstore. Local reports of the time indicated that Mr. Whitlock was often too indisposed, due to his affection for strong drink, to light the beacon and his wife tended to the light more than he did.

It was in 1902 when the lighthouse engineer first recommended the purchase of more land at the site. However this required several more letters of recommendation before the plan was approved. In 1906 the light on the tree was replaced with a lantern hung from a post. Although there was a small house at the site that the lamp lighter lived in, it was most likely not owned by the government.

Finally, in 1908 the government purchased additional land at the site and by 1910 a full-fledged light station was completed with a new tower, keeper's house, and other buildings.

After numerous complaints the government added a fog bell to the site in December of 1930 when a new pyramid style fog bell tower was built. When new technology became available, in 1959 the fog bell was removed from the lighthouse.

In 1931 the Superintendent recommended that the lens color be changed from red to white. However he quickly changed his mind and suggested that the light be changed to green, since there were several other white Canadian lights in the area. It was also in 1931 that electricity was finally brought to the lighthouse and the keeper's dwelling.

Eventually automation arrived at the lighthouse and the keepers were no longer needed. The 4th order Fresnel lens was removed from the tower in 1969 and replaced by a modern optic. The original lens is now on display at the lighthouse museum in Rockland, Maine. In 1977, the keeper's house was deeded to the Washington County Vocational Technical Institute. They eventually sold the property and the keeper's house became privately owned.

In 1998, under the Maine Lights Program, ownership of the tower was transferred to the St. Croix Historical Society.

WHITLOCK LIGHT, ST. CROIX RIVER.

This vintage post card of Whitlock's Mill Lighthouse from the water shows the tower with its unpainted natural brownish-red color and the lantern room was painted green. The tower was later painted white and for many years the lantern room was painted red. Today the lantern room is painted black.

Aerial view of Whitlock's Mill Lighthouse when it was an active lighthouse station.

View from the lantern room at Whitlock's Mill Lighthouse looking over the St. Croix River. Photograph by Chuck Petronis, U.S. Coast Guard.

Inside the tower at Whitlock's Mill Lighthouse. Photograph by Chuck Petronis, U.S. Coast Guard.

Three of the primary buildings at Whitlock's Mill Lighthouse. The small stone building was the oil house, where oil and other types of fuel were stored. The pyramid building once held a fog bell. Photo by Ron Foster.

Edgar Wallace of Jonesport, Maine, was a Coast Guard lighthouse keeper at Whitlock's Mill from 1947 to 1950. Photograph courtesy of Myron & Nancy Wallace.

Whitlock's Mill Lighthouse was the last station where keeper Jasper L. Cheney served, retiring from service here in 1957. Cheney, born in Canada in 1893, became a naturalized U.S. citizen and joined the Coast Guard in 1928. However, in 1931 he joined the United States Lighthouse Service and was first stationed as a lighthouse keeper at Rockland Breakwater Lighthouse. Two years later he was transferred to Libby Island Lighthouse. In 1939, while stationed at Libby Island, he found himself again back in the Coast Guard when the Lighthouse Service was dissolved and merged into the Coast Guard. He remained at Libby Island until 1949 when he was able to secure the position as keeper at Whitlock's Mill Lighthouse. He retired from the Coast Guard in 1957.

Cheney's daughter, Ella, had the honored privilege of being married at Whitlock's Mill Lighthouse in 1953. Ella recalled that her parents loved Whitlock's Mill Lighthouse and they worked tirelessly to make the station a place of beauty, inside and out. Ella recalled in a story in *Lighthouse Digest*, "Many, many tourists visited in the summer and all agreed that it was just breathtaking with all the flowers in bloom and the scenery." Photograph courtesy of Jeff Robinson.

BMC Russell Reilly had a long and distinguished career in the Coast Guard. He served three separate times as a Coast Guard keeper at Little River Lighthouse. He also served at West Quoddy, Libby Island and Mt. Desert lighthouses, as well as on the Pollock Rip Lightship. The Coast Guard rarely keeps anyone at one location very long and such was the case with Reilly, who also served at the Coast Guard Headquarters in Washington, DC and at the Lifeboat Stations at Quoddy Head and Cross Island. However, his assignment to Whitlock's Mill Lighthouse was his favorite. It was the only assignment where his family was allowed to live with him.

His daughter, Kelly, who was a pre-schooler at the time, still has fond memories, years later, of their life at the lighthouse. She got to spend her days with her father while her mother was at work and her sister and brother were off to school. She said she followed her father everywhere as he did his daily checks on the station. She remembers how he used to say, as they climbed the winding steps of the tower, how important it was to make sure that the light was in working order and that everything must always be clean and spotless. In the wintertime her Dad would pull her on the sled up the long curving driveway to the top of the hill to collect the mail. Then they both rode the sled down the driveway and around the curves back home. Generally, at noon they sat in the recliner and watched a movie together. It was always a race for who could say "end of the movie," first.

Although Reilly was honored with a number of important awards and medals during his career, to his daughter, Kelly, he was a loving father. Photograph courtesy of Kelly Reilly.

The fog bell from Whitlock's Mill Lighthouse was removed from the lighthouse in 1959 and is now on display at the St. Croix Historical Society. Shown here with the fog bell in 2001 is Doris Smith Fuchs who is the great granddaughter of Aaron Tucker who was a lighthouse keeper at Whitlock's Mill Lighthouse. Photograph courtesy of Jacqueline Flint.

Whitlock's Mill Lighthouse with its idyllic setting on the St. Croix River. Photograph courtesy of the National Archives.

Two unidentified lighthouse keepers pose by the fog bell tower at Whitlock's Mill.

Poet Lauriat of the Lighthouse Service

Frederic W. Morong, Jr.
1883-1947

Lighthouse Service District Machinist Frederic W. Morong, Jr. wrote the most famous poem in lighthouse history at the kitchen table in the keeper's house at Little River Lighthouse in Cutler, Maine.

Morong was no stranger to lighthouses. Born on April 17, 1883 at Grand Manan, New Brunswick, Canada, he was the son of lighthouse keeper Frederic William. Morong, Sr. and Ellen Douglas Campbell of Calais, Maine.

He attended school in Lubec and later at Washington Academy in East Machias. Although he left the area for a time, he returned to Lubec to seek work locally and be closer to other family members. As a talented musician, he belonged to the Lubec Band Association and Lubec Brass Band. He married Maude Louise Libby of Vinalhaven, Maine on June 26, 1907.

He joined the U.S. Lighthouse Service in 1922 and started as a mechanic and worked his way up through the ranks, as District Machinist and later as an Inspector.

During the time he was the District Machinist, he traveled to many of the lighthouses and often stayed overnight at the stations. By doing so, he became good friends with many lighthouse keepers and their families.

Dave Gamage, whose grandfather was a keeper at Matinicus Rock Lighthouse and Whitehead Lighthouse recalled his grandfather's recollection of Morong saying that they always enjoyed his visits. He also said that Morong could fix anything that moved and if he didn't have the right fittings, he would make them.

In those days, much of the equipment at lighthouses was made of brass. This was not limited to the machinery required to operate the light and fog bell. The lens was encased with brass fittings and everything from oil cans to dust pans, was made of brass, all which required constant cleaning and polishing. Everything that was brass was always required to be shining every single day.

Morong had heard the complaints about polishing the brass, first as a child from his father and then from every lighthouse keeper along the coast. He especially heard of the complaints when he would arrive to repair the machinery and get grease on the brass.

One day while at Little River Lighthouse, after a day of extremely hard work, he ended the day relaxing with the family of lighthouse keeper Willie Corbett. Although they often played some music and sang some songs, this day, the discussion jokingly got around to brass. So, Morong got some paper and pencil and proceeded to sit at the kitchen table saying he needed to write something humorous about brass. Exactly how long it to took him to compose the work is unclear, but in later years, Neil Corbett, son of light keeper Willie Corbett, would recall how everyone was gathered around to hear the first reading of Morong's work.

Somehow or another, the poem eventually was read on a popular Boston radio program and circulated widely to all light stations in the United States.

Over the years the poem has often been recited at lighthouse events and even used at modern Coast Guard events. However, in some of these writings, people and officials have changed a few words, namely, changing "beat on wife," to "holler at wife," or "scream at wife." However, many old timers have stated that the expression, "beat on wife," should not be taken literally, as it was an expression which meant to be "complaining loudly," and not meant to refer to any type of physical abuse, which was nearly unheard of in the Lighthouse Service.

When Morong retired, he and his wife lived in South Portland where he was an active member in many volunteer organizations. He died at the age of 64 on December 23, 1947, and was interred at the Carver Cemetery at Vinalhaven, Maine.

IT'S BRASSWORK

By Frederic W. Morong, Jr.

Oh what is the bane of a lightkeeper's life
That causes him worry, struggle and strife,
That makes him use cuss words and beat on his wife?
It's BRASSWORK

What makes him look ghastly consumptive and thin,
What robs him of health, vigor and vim,
And causes despair and drives him to sin?
It's BRASSWORK

The devil himself could never invent,
A material causing more world wide lament,
And in Uncle Sam's service about ninety percent
Is BRASSWORK

The lamp in the tower, reflector and shade,
The tools and accessories pass in the parade,
As a matter of fact the whole outfit is made
Of BRASSWORK

The oil containers I polish until
My poor back is broken, aching and still,
Each gallon, each quart, each pint and gill
Is BRASSWORK

I lay down to slumber all weary and sore,
I walk in my sleep, I awake with a snore,
And I'm shining the knob on my bedchamber door
That BRASSWORK

From pillar to post rags and polish I tote,
I'm never without them, for you will please note,
That even the buttons I wear on my coat,
Are BRASSWORK

The machinery, clockwork, and fog signal bell,
The coal hods, the dustpans, the pump in the well,
No I'll leave it to you mates...If this isn't...well,
BRASSWORK

I dig, scrub and polish, and work with a might,
And just when I get it all shining and bright,
In come the fog like a thief in the night,
Goodbye BRASSWORK

Frederic W. Morong, Jr.

I start the next day when noontime draws near,
A boatload of summer visitors appear,
For no other reason than to smooch and besmear,
My BRASSWORK

So it goes along all summer, and along in the fall,
Comes the district machinists to overhaul,
and rub dirty paws all over,
My BRASSWORK

And again in the spring, if per chance it may be,
An efficiency star is awarded to me,
I open the package and what do I see?
More BRASSWORK

Oh, why should the spirit of mortal be proud,
In the short span of life that he is allowed,
If all the lining in every dark cloud,
Is BRASSWORK

And when I have polished until I am cold,
And I have taken my oath to the Heavenly fold,
Will my harp and my crown be made of pure gold?
No! BRASSWORK

Father of the Coast Guard

Hopley Yeaton
1740-1812

Hopley Yeaton, one of America's early military heroes, and a man few probably know or have heard of, was once buried in Maine's Washington County.

When Hopley Yeaton retired, at the age of 70, he settled on a farm in North Lubec. During his retirement, he was active in community affairs, including the incorporation of the town of Lubec. Being a member of the Masonic Lodge, he helped establish a Masonic Chapter in Eastport. He died on May 12, 1812.

The flag draped casket of Hopley Yeaton at the small cemetery in North Lubec before it was removed and placed on board the Coast Guard Cutter Eagle for transport to New London Connecticut. Photograph courtesy of Shirley Morong.

However, before his retirement to Lubec, in his official position as the first commissioned sea going officer under the Constitution of the newly formed government of United States, he had urged the government to build a lighthouse at West Quoddy Head, which they finally did during the last year of his service, 1809.

In 1974, government officials decided that his grave, which had been located in a small cemetery behind a private dwelling in North Lubec should be exhumed and that Hopley's remains would be moved to a place of prominent distinction at the Coast Guard Academy in New London, Connecticut.

On November 1, 1974, five Coast Guard Academy cadets, a few Coast Guard officers, a Lubec undertaker, an undertaker from New London, and several onlookers watched as the cadets armed with shovels, spades and a pickaxe, began to dig on a straight line behind the gravestone.

As the excavation reached the four-foot depth, the son of the Lubec undertaker probed the dirt with an iron bar and struck what seemed to be wood. Using a spade, he removed enough dirt to enable the anxious watchers to see what appeared to be the top of a wooden box. The cadets continued to dig until the whole shape of the all-wooden box was exposed. The two undertakers decided it would not be feasible to try to remove the casket in one piece so the cover, which was just laid over it, was handed to the cadets. It was in excellent condition, thought to be made of pine, and the inner side of it resembled a smooth, beautifully grained counter top recently finished.

Human bones, which were visible in the water-filled casket were removed by the undertakers and placed in a plastic bag to be preserved. The remains of the coffin were taken up in pieces.

Late that afternoon the remains of Captain Yeaton were placed in a concrete vault and buried in a grave at West Quoddy Lighthouse to remain while a suitable monument could be established at the Coast Guard Academy.

August 19, 1975 was an exciting day in Lubec. The Coast Guard Training Ship *Eagle* had arrived the night before and was anchored in Johnson's Bay where it was visible by many residents. She was there to take the remains of Hopley Yeaton to the Coast Guard Academy.

The officials then removed the remains from the temporary grave at West Quoddy Head Light and brought them back, in a flag draped casket, to the original gravesite in North Lubec for a special service.

Shortly before 10:00 am about 200 people, including 75 cadets from the *Eagle* as well as Coast Guard officials from the Academy and the First Coast Guard District, gathered to partake in a brief ceremony that was opened with a prayer by Chaplain Frederick K. Brink, who also spoke of the important role that Captain Yeaton played during his years of service in patrolling the coast against

The five Coast Guard cadets who removed the remains of Hopley Yeaton from his burial place in North Lubec. Photograph courtesy of Shirley Morong.

smugglers. Then, Rear Admiral James P. Steward, Commander of the First Coast Guard District in Boston, read aloud the story of the life of Hopley Yeaton. Following the closing prayer, the casket was lifted by six cadets from its resting place near a new stone plaque that had been placed over the original gravesite by the Coast Guard. It was carried along the dirt road to the pier down

Onlookers peer into the ground at the casket of Hopley Yeaton, just before his remains were removed. Photograph courtesy of the Lubec Historical Society. The epitaph on the tombstone says:

No Joys Domestic, Nor Love Of Ease
Could Cool His Patriot Zeal
In War or Peace

on the shore where it was placed on board the Coast Guard cutter *Point Hannon* from Jonesport to transfer to the *Eagle*. Two platoons of cadets followed the casket bearers accompanied by the beat of drums.

Later that afternoon, the *Eagle* sailed by West Quoddy Head Lighthouse with all sails up bound for the Academy and Yeaton's final resting place.

A few months later, on Sunday, October 19, 1975, a small group of Lubec residents traveled to New London Connecticut to attend the ceremony of the dedication of the new monument placed on the final grave of Captain Hopley Yeaton at the Coast Guard Academy. An impressive service was held in the Memorial chapel with speak-

This old Coast Guard photo shows the casket of Hopley Yeaton being hoisted onboard the Coast Guard Cutter Eagle, in Lubec, Maine, to be transported to its new burial site at the Coast Guard Academy in New London, Connecticut. Courtesy of the Lubec Historical Society.

ers representing various branches of the Armed forces, the Masonic Lodge and friends and relatives from Yeaton's home state of New Hampshire. The National Anthem was played by the U.S. Coast Guard Band and the anthem "God Who Heard Our Father's Voice" was sung by the Coast Guard Academy Idlers. The benediction was given by Commander Norman A. Ricard, Academy Chaplain.

This was followed by a ribbon cutting ceremony by the square box-like stone monument to Hopley Yeaton, which is on a grassy knoll next to the Coast Guard Chapel.

Hopley Yeaton was born near Portsmouth, New Hampshire in 1740 and went to sea at an early age. He became a merchant captain as a young man and saw service in the Continental Navy during the War for Independence in 1776. He was active with the Sons of Liberty, served as an officer onboard the Continental Frigates *Raleigh* and *Deane*, and commanded the cutters

The dedication ceremony at the new tomb of Hopley Yeaton on the grounds of the Coast Guard Academy in New London, Connecticut. Photograph courtesy of Shirley Morong.

Scammel, New Hampshire, and *Governor Gilman* of the U.S. Revenue Cutter Service.

It is important to remember here that at the conclusion of the Revolutionary War, the Continental Navy, Marines and Army were disbanded, leaving the U.S. without a regular military force. Then, on August 4, 1790, Congress authorized the creation of the United States Revenue Marine, which changed its name in 1862 to the Revenue Cutter Service. When the United States Revenue Marine was formed in 1790, with ten vessels to insure that import tariffs were collected to finance the new government, they were in effect the only military sea going vessels of the new government until the U.S. Navy was authorized and formed by Congress a few years later.

In 1915, Congress directed that the United States Revenue Cutter Service and the United States Life Saving Service be merged to form one organization that would be named the United States Coast Guard. Because the United States Coast Guard is a direct descendant of the United States Revenue Marine the Coast Guard has the distinction of being the oldest continually serving military organization of the five armed services and the first to hold the title of "United States." In 1939, the United States Lighthouse Service was dissolved and its duties were merged into the United States Coast Guard.

On March 21, 1791, President George Washington appointed Hopley Yeaton as the first sea-going officer of the United States. His commission was signed by both George Washington and Thomas Jefferson and he was assigned to command the Revenue Marine cutter *Scammel* for patrol duty along the coast from New Hampshire to Calais, Maine. Widespread smuggling and piracy were a constant and growing menace along the entire length of the coastal area and Captain Yeaton was involved in many serious encounters.

As well as successfully enforcing maritime law along the sea border with Canada, he was the first to propose formal training of young men for service aboard cutters.

And that's why the United States of America named Hopley Yeaton, a man who served his county well, who spent a good portion of his life in Maine's Sunrise County, and was at one time buried here as the "Father of the Coast Guard."

Revenue Ensign and Pennant

First Lady of Light

Connie Scovill Small
June 4, 1901 – January 25, 2005

A book on the lighthouses of Maine's Washington County could not be complete without a separate chapter honoring the memory of Connie Scovill Small who was known in history circles as Maine's "First Lady of Light."

From 1920 to 1948, Connie and her husband Elson tended lighthouses along the Maine and New Hampshire Coast and many of those lighthouses were in Washington County Maine, including Lubec Channel Lighthouse, St. Croix River Lighthouse, and Avery Rock Lighthouse.

She and her husband not only lived the lighthouse life, but other members of their extended family also established themselves in maritime history with their dedication to save and protect the lives of those at sea. Connie's maternal grandmother was a governess at West Quoddy Head Lighthouse and was married at the lighthouse. Her father was a member of the original crew at West Quoddy Life Boat Station and later served as the Head Keeper there. Loring Myers, keeper at Lubec Channel Lighthouse was her uncle, and later Connie's husband served as the keeper of that same lighthouse. Connie's sister, Minnie, married lighthouse keeper Charles W. Allen who served at Avery Rock Lighthouse. Later, Connie and her husband also served as the keepers of that same lighthouse.

During her lighthouse life, Connie learned what self-reliance was all about. She said, "You had to be self confident, independent and have lots of spunk and courage to run a lighthouse. You also had to at times be able to conquer loneliness and at times a feeling of being forsaken."

At 83 years old she wrote the bestselling book, *The Lighthouse Keeper's Wife,* which has helped to preserve much of our lighthouse history that otherwise might have been lost forever. By the time she was 100 years old, she had given over 600 lectures, something she continued to do right up to a few weeks before she died at the age of 103.

The one message she stressed in all those lectures was that, while it was vital to save the lighthouse structures themselves, it was more vitally important to save the stories, the memories and the photographs of the keepers and the families who lived at the lighthouses. "Without the stories and the memories," she said, "the lighthouses are just empty hollow structures. But with the stories and memories they come to life for generations to come." In one of the last letters she wrote, which was duplicated and sent to a number of people, she stated, *" I have now given up my work with lighthouses and passed it on to groups of wonderful people who will carry on the tradition and love of lighthouses as much as I do. I hope that some of the beauty will linger with you."*

Connie Small's father, Ira Elroy Scovill (1864-1930), was one of the original crew and later the head keeper at the U.S. Life Saving Service West Quoddy Life Boat Station.

The West Quoddy Life Boat Station where Connie's father was the head keeper. The U.S. Life Saving Service was the sister organization of the United States Light House Service. In the early days, the word lighthouse was two separate words. The Life Saving Service became the Coast Guard in 1915 and in 1939 the Lighthouse Service was dissolved and merged into the Coast Guard. Photograph circa 1915.

Connie Small's parents in front of the West Quoddy Life Saving Service Station.

Connie Small took this photograph on her first visit to Lubec Channel Lighthouse as the wife of a lighthouse keeper. During the time that Elson and Connie were engaged, Elson was serving an as officer on a ship and was gone for long periods of time. The last time he returned, he told Connie that he had been offered the job of an assistant lighthouse keeper, and as told in Connie's book, he asked her, "Do you love me enough to go with me to a lighthouse?" They were married on November 23, 1920.

Lighthouse keeper Elson Small and cousin Emma Davis in the station boat at Lubec Channel Lighthouse in 1921. Connie Small took the photo.

After serving at Maine lighthouses for 28 years, Connie and Elson Small enjoyed there retirement years. Elson loved to play the banjo. Lighthouse keeper Elson Small died in 1960.

During the planning of the 2001 annual American Lighthouse Foundation fund raising weekend, Tim Harrison, who was president of the group at that time, suggested that the evening's dinner also be a 100th birthday party for Connie Small. Connie was asked to attend and she graciously agreed. However, she had no idea at the time how many people would show up for the event. On the day of the big party, she was amazed to see two uniformed Coast Guard officers in a limousine arrive to pick her up. At 100 years old, this was her first ride in a limo and she commented on how big it was. Photograph by Paula Roberts.

Connie was all smiles as she stood in the entryway to the banquet room, filled with over 300 people, as her long time friend Bill Thomson introduced her for her 100th birthday party in June of 2001. Senior Chief Tom Dutton, USCG, and Chief Petty Officer Mark Cutter, USCG, escorted her to the banquet hall and to her table. *Lighthouse Digest* archives photograph.

Color Guard at Connie Small's 100th Birthday Celebration on June 3, 2001.

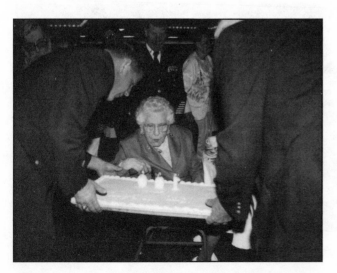

No one knew what she wished for, but Connie Small blew out all the candles of her 100th birthday cake at the same time. Photograph by Paula Roberts.

Loving to talk about lighthouses, Connie did not hesitate to take the microphone at her 100th birthday party, not only to thank everyone but she urged them to carry on the task to save the stories and memories.

Connie Small loved to meet people, share her stories, and autograph copies of her book as she did at a breakfast held the day following her 100th birthday party sponsored by the American Lighthouse Foundation.

The day following her big 100th birthday party, Connie visited the Portsmouth Light House Station in New Hampshire, where she and her husband were last stationed. She took a moment to pose here with Tim Harrison, far left, Kathleen Finnegan and Bill Thomson. Bill, a noted lighthouse historian and author, had met Connie back in the 1940s. Tim and Kathleen first met Connie in 1992.

As the day winded down, Connie took Tim's hand and looked him squarely in the eyes and said, "Tim, I have your first issue of *Lighthouse Digest,* you know, the one with the newspaper print, and now look how it looks today. I used to have trouble sleeping at night worrying about who will continue to keep alive the memories of the lighthouse keepers and their families, and who will keep telling their stories so they will not be forgotten. As I looked around that room last night and saw all those people, [referring to those in attendance at her 100th birthday party sponsored by the American Lighthouse Foundation] and how you brought all this together, I know that I don't have to worry anymore." Photograph by Paula Roberts.

At 101 years old, Connie Small poses here for this photograph with the author. Connie Small is holding one of the lighthouse books Harrison authored, *The Golden Age of American Lighthouses.* And Harrison is holding Connie's book, *The Lighthouse Keeper's Wife.*

On that day, in the front of her book, Connie wrote, *"To Tim Harrison, a wonderful friend of mine and of lighthouses. May the sunrise give Hope and Inspiration, and the sunset the comfort of a day well spent. Many Blessings, Connie Small."*

Lady of Light

By Patricia (Patty) Martin

Her thoughts—poetic beauty spoke to me
of days gone by,
Her life a "lighthouse" in itself
For us to somehow steer by...

Getting to know this one true gem
Through stories told by coal-burned fire,
How sad to see that light go out,
Of which I'd never tire,

So, Connie as you leave this earth
Move on towards distant shore,
Remember, we know your love of life
The history of your lore,
You inspired me, this little one
To lift my lamp on high,

Though not a lighthouse keeper's wife,
I know that I will try...
To tell the lighthouse tales we know
And share our own adventures,
In all events and places we go,

As members and activators!
So, Connie...as you cross that bar,
And look back towards the shore,

Know that you've left a legacy of light,
We hope to treasure it more!

When the American Lighthouse Foundation and *Lighthouse Digest* sent out notices announcing that Connie Small had passed away at the age of 103, tributes came in from around the world. In her memory, far away from the Maine and New Hampshire coast where Connie lived and served, the flag at Georgia's Tybee Island Lighthouse was flown at half-staff.

Never again will lighthouse life, as it was in the days of the lighthouse keepers, be repeated. We wonder what Connie Small could
have been thinking about on this day in 1921, as she and her cousin
Emma Davis walked away in the drizzling rain after visiting
Connie's husband, Elson, at the Lubec Channel Lighthouse.

From the family photo albums . . .

Lightship duty was considered the most dangerous of all assignments of the United States Lighthouse Service and the United States Coast Guard. Lightships were basically floating lighthouses that were stationed at a position where it was considered to dangerous or to expensive to build a lighthouse.

Capt. George K. Martin was a veteran lightship captain under the United States Lighthouse Service. All of his dates of service and locations are not known at this time. However, he served as captain of the Pollock Rip Lightship LV 110, from 1924 to 1925, the Portland (Maine) Lightship from 1925 to 1927, the Hen & Chickens Lightship, possibly from 1932 to 1933 and the Cross Rip Lightship sometime in 1937 or thereafter.

For many years Capt. Martin wore the uniform of the United States Lighthouse Service, however when the Lighthouse Service was merged into the Coast Guard in 1939 he transferred to the Coast Guard. He is shown here in 1939 from a photograph taken in Lubec, Maine wearing his new Coast Guard uniform.

Since lightships were never stationed in the waters off the coast of Downeast Maine, it is unclear why this photograph was taken in Lubec. He might have spent later years serving at one of the areas Coast Guard stations or retired in the Lubec area.

Family stories state that Alvah Hooper, shown here in his younger years served at one of the lighthouses or life-saving stations in Downeast Maine. Photograph courtesy Donna Michaud.

Alvah Hooper and his wife in later years. Photograph courtesy of Donna Michaud.

John T. Holmes is shown here wearing some type of a seafaring cap. Although he never served as a full time lighthouse keeper, it is believed that he did act as an unofficial relief keeper at several lighthouses. Unfortunately, very little is known about John T. Holmes, as is the case with many old photographs.

An unidentified lighthouse keeper believed to be from Washington County.

1789 - 1939

Epilogue

It was modernization that was the beginning of the end for lighthouses and the keepers and family members who served at them.

The old United States Lighthouse Service was an organization of people that were proud of their history and their tradition. They were a different breed of people, from the keepers to the engineers, from the watchmen to the laborers, from the office employees to the crews of the lighthouse tenders and lightships and especially the family members. But as modernization crept forward, it was the beginning of the end for the lighthouse keepers and their way of life.

Automation of some lighthouses and the removal of their keepers and families happened early on at some stations, generally because the usefulness of the lighthouse had diminished with a loss of an industry, drop in population or less traveled shipping lanes.

But the ultimate end came in 1939 when President Roosevelt's reorganization of federal agencies dissolved the United States Lighthouse Service and merged it into the United States Coast Guard, an act that had been opposed by many.

Lighthouse Service employees were given the option of remaining on as civilian employees or joining the Coast Guard. For the most part they split evenly in their decisions. Although the Coast Guard sent out letters and issued bulletins welcoming its new employees, animosity soon grew against the Coast Guard, especially when orders came from Washington to destroy everything that that had the name or the logo of the U.S. Lighthouse Service on it.

Items such as the dinnerware featuring the logo of the U.S. Lighthouse Service were smashed on the rocks, and everything from dustpans to toilet paper holders, flags, and all types of brass items were burned, buried or tossed out at sea. Generally, what was saved, was saved by the lighthouse keepers and their family members or simply overlooked.

In those early days some of the Coast Guardsmen sent to lighthouse had great respect for the old lighthouse service employees, but others did not, and many in command could not wait to get rid of the old echelon once and for all. Some commanders tried to keep up the tradition started by the lighthouse service and others would have no part of it. As the new Coast Guard emerged after World War II, with the exception of few officers, there was for the most part, no respect or care for many of the lighthouses, the keeper's homes or the history of the organization they had taken over. Old documents and photographs, which would now be valuable artifacts today, but also an important part of recorded history, were simply tossed in dumpsters or left at lighthouses for the taking of anyone that wanted them.

It wasn't until many years later that the Coast Guard would even acknowledge the error of their ways, and changed their attitude but by then the real damage had been done. If it had not been for a small group of dedicated Coast Guard officers scattered around the country, even more history would have been lost.

There are many accounts, too many to mention here, of the feelings expressed by some of the old lighthouse service. But one example came from Connie Small, Maine's "First Lady of Light," who with her husband, Elson, served as lighthouse keepers on the Maine coast for 28 years. A short time after his retirement in June of 1949, he decided to go back to the last lighthouse that had been their family station and was now occupied by Coast Guardsmen. He found the station already had not been properly cared for, and the house, once kept tidy and neat was a mess and looked more like a military barracks without an officer in charge. She said, "Elson went up to the tower. He found the lenscover on the floor where the station crew had been walking on it. It almost broke his heart." He never returned to the lighthouse and died 11 years later.

In the late 1970s, Connie decided she would go back to the lighthouse again, hoping to rekindle some lighthouse memories. She even called the Coast Guard to get permission. When she arrived she saw the house in such disrepair, and a crew of men that made her feel so awkward and embarrassed, that she left without even climbing the tower that she had loved so much.

In later years she would return again, but this time she was treated like royalty, the Coast Guard had changed, this time, she felt, for the better. And she was proud of the Coast Guard men and women she met.

Some of our lighthouses no longer stand, others, where the tower still stands, the keeper's home is gone, and only a few light stations still have the entire lighthouse station intact. It is now the responsibility of the next generation of caretakers and preservationists to assure that these lighthouses and the history associated with them are saved and protected, so that future generations can understand how we arrived at where we are today.

TRANSPLANTED

(Retirement of a Lighthouse Keeper)

By Catherine Freeman Thaxter
Daughter of lighthouse keeper James Freeman

My father left his lonely isle to live
Where Waves break only in a field of grain,
Exchanged the sea gull for the meadowlark,
The lashing spray, for gentle inland rain.

He worked his land with energy and pride,
Exulting in a fertileness' unknown
Among the granite, barren ways that marked
Those few, wind-tortured acres he'd called home.

Yet evenings, when the talk would turn to seeds,
To things that landlocked minds beat understood,
His jackknife moved in rhythm with his voice
To whittle dories out of kindling wood.

About the Author

As one of the nation's leading lighthouse preservationists and historians, this is the seventh lighthouse book that Timothy Harrison has written or co-authored.

Harrison is the co-founder and editor of *Lighthouse Digest* magazine, was the co-founder of Lighthouse Depot, "The World's Largest Lighthouse Gift Store," the Lighthouse Depot Catalog, and the Lighthouse Depot Explorer Data Base. In 1992 he co-founded the non-profit New England Lighthouse Foundation that later became the American Lighthouse Foundation, which he was president of, from 1994 to 2007. Harrison was also the primary creator of the American Lighthouse Foundation's, Museum of Lighthouse History that in 2007 was merged into the Maine Lighthouse Museum in Rockland, Maine.

Harrison says his interest was inspired by a chance meeting with the late Ken Black, a retired Coast Guardsman, known by many as "Mr. Lighthouse," who founded the Shore Village Museum that later became the Maine Lighthouse Museum. Since starting in the "lighthouse business" Harrison has spent years researching lighthouse history, mostly from old documents at local historical societies and libraries around the county, as well as at museums and visiting with former lighthouse keepers and descendants of lighthouse keepers. He says he probably every lighthouse book ever printed and searches the Internet, bookstores, and antique shops for old newspaper stories, magazine articles and other material. Having written hundreds of stories about lighthouses, he says he prefers to write stories about lighthouses using material from actual memories, old documents, and accounts written at the time, as well as from memories of lighthouse keepers and their descendants.

Although Harrison now limits his speaking engagements, he has spoken to hundreds of audiences around the United States and Canada, with the largest crowd being over 3,000 people at the relighting of Clark's Point Lighthouse in New Bedford, MA. He also spoke at the largest gathering in history of descendants of the keeper's of one lighthouse, at North Carolina's Cape Hatteras Lighthouse Keeper's Descendants Homecoming.

Harrison has traveled and visited lighthouses all over North America and is a sought-after expert on lighthouse history and preservation by the media and has been quoted and interviewed by numerous newspapers and radio stations. He has also appeared on national television broadcasts such as CNN and ABC-TV's Nightline, as well as on many local TV programs such as Made in Maine and Bill Green's Maine.

It was Harrison's initiative to have the American Lighthouse Foundation host an International Lighthouse Convention that would focus on educating the younger generation about lighthouses and preservation. The successful Convention, that was held in New Bedford, Massachusetts, drew lighthouse historians and preservationists from around the world. He is also an original supporter of the annual Great Lakes Lighthouse Festival, held in Alpena, Michigan, and has donated artifacts from his personal collection to their museum.

Harrison was a member of the first team of volunteers of The American Lighthouse Foundation to assess the condition of Little River Lighthouses and has participated in the actual labor at Little River as part of the restoration project at the light station. He negotiated with the Coast Guard to have a beacon reinstalled in the tower, planned the relighting ceremony and was its Master of Ceremonies. As an unpaid volunteer, he personally prepared the application for ownership of the Little River Lighthouse for the American Lighthouse Foundation, under the National Historic Lighthouse Preservation Act of 2000, for which the National Trust for Historic Preservation presented an award. He now serves as co-chairman of the Friends of Little River Lighthouse, which is a chapter of the American Lighthouse Foundation.

Harrison has been the recipient of numerous awards from many organizations including The Founders Award and the Presidents Award from North Carolina's the Outer Banks Lighthouse Society and the Great Lakes Lighthouse Award. His most coveted honor was bestowed him in September of 2005, when Rear Admiral David Petoske, Commander of the First Coast Guard District, surprised him at a ceremony, by presenting him with the United States Coast Guard's Meritorious Public Service Commendation Award and Medal.

Harrison has a true love for lighthouses and the preservation of their history and a burning desire to save them for future generations. For many years he has stressed in talks, presentations and interviews saying, *"It's important to remember that lighthouses were built for one purpose only, to save lives; now it's our turn to save the lighthouses."*

Non Profit Lighthouse Groups in Washington County, Maine

Friends of Little River Lighthouse
A Chapter of the American Lighthouse Foundation
P.O. Box 671
East Machias, ME 04630
www.LittleRiverLight.org
Phone: (207) 259-3833

Friends of Nash Island Lighthouse
P.O. Box 250
Addison, ME 04606

West Quoddy Head Light Keepers Association
P.O. Box 378
Lubec, ME 04652
www.WestQuoddy.com
Phone: (207) 733-2180

To learn more about lighthouses, we
recommend that you subscribe to

Lighthouse
DIGEST

"The Magazine of Lighthouses"

Lighthouse Digest
P.O. Box 250
East Machias, ME 04630
(207) 259-2121
www.LighthouseDigest.net